The Architecture of Security in the Asia-Pacific

The Architecture of Security in the Asia-Pacific

EDITED BY RON HUISKEN

E PRESS

Published by ANU E Press
The Australian National University
Canberra ACT 0200, Australia
Email: anuepress@anu.edu.au
This title is also available online at: http://epress.anu.edu.au/architecture_citation.html

National Library of Australia
Cataloguing-in-Publication entry

Title: The architecture of security in the Asia-Pacific / editor Ron Huisken.

ISBN: 9781921666025 (pbk.) 9781921666032 (pdf.)

Subjects: National security--Asia--Congresses.
National security--Pacific Area--Congresses.

Other Authors/Contributors:
Huisken, R. H. (Ronald Herman), 1946-
Australian National University. Strategic and Defence Studies Centre.
China Foundation for International and Strategic Studies.

Dewey Number: 355.33095

All rights reserved. No part of this publication may be reproduced, stored in a retrieval system or transmitted in any form or by any means, electronic, mechanical, photocopying or otherwise, without the prior permission of the publisher.

The *Canberra Papers on Strategy and Defence* series is a collection of publications arising principally from research undertaken at the SDSC. Canberra Papers have been peer reviewed since 2006. All Canberra Papers are available for sale: visit the SDSC website at <http://rspas.anu.edu.au/sdsc/canberra_papers.php> for abstracts and prices. Electronic copies (in pdf format) of most SDSC Working Papers published since 2002 may be downloaded for free from the SDSC website at <http://rspas.anu.edu.au/sdsc/working_papers.php>. The entire Working Papers series is also available on a 'print on demand' basis.

Strategic and Defence Studies Centre Publications Program Advisory Review Panel: Emeritus Professor Paul Dibb; Professor Desmond Ball; Professor David Horner; Professor Hugh White; Professor William Tow; Professor Anthony Milner; Professor Virginia Hooker; Dr Coral Bell; Dr Pauline Kerr

Strategic and Defence Studies Centre Publications Program Editorial Board: Professor Hugh White; Dr Brendan Taylor; Dr Christian Enemark; Miss Meredith Thatcher (series editor)

Cover design by ANU E Press

This edition © 2009 ANU E Press

Table of Contents

Contributors	vii
Acronyms and Abbreviations	xi
List of Tables	xiii
1. Introduction Ron Huisken	1
2. Developing East Asia's Security Architecture: An Australian perspective on ASEAN processes Brendan Taylor	11
3. The ASEAN Power Zhai Kun	21
4. The SCO's Success in Security Architecture Pan Guang	33
5. Shifting Tides: China and North Korea Zhu Feng	45
6. 'The Six-Party Talks Process: Towards an Asian Concert?' Robert Ayson	59
7. The US Role in the Future Security Architecture for East Asia Ron Huisken	67
8. The Role of the United States in the Future Security Architecture for East Asia—from the Perspective of China-US Military-to-Military Interaction Lu Dehong	85
9. Potential Strategic Risks in China-US Relations Yuan Peng	101
10. Changes in China-Japan Relations and East Asian Security Zhang Tuosheng	111
Index	121

Contributors

Robert Ayson directs The Australian National University's Graduate Studies in Strategy and Defence program and is a Fellow in the Strategic and Defence Studies Centre. He has taught in New Zealand universities and served as adviser to the New Zealand parliamentary select committee on Foreign Affairs, Defence and Trade. The author of *Thomas Schelling and the Nuclear Age*, Frank Cass, London and New York, 2004, his research interests include strategic concepts, Asia-Pacific stability, and Australia-New Zealand defence issues.

Ron Huisken is senior fellow at the Strategic and Defence Studies Centre, The Australian National University. He has held a variety of research and teaching positions in Australia and overseas, together with assignments in the United Nations and the Australian Public Service. He spent a number of years with the Stockholm International Peace Research Institute working particularly on military expenditures, naval forces and nuclear arms control. At the UN Department of Disarmament Affairs, he played a key role in producing a landmark study on the relationships between disarmament and development. In government in Australia, he worked predominantly on arms control issues with the Department of Foreign Affairs and Trade and on alliance management questions with the Department of Defence. He also served as deputy Chief of Mission in the Australian embassy in Bonn in 1990–94. He returned to academia in 2001 where his research interests include East Asian security, alliance politics, and proliferation. His publications include (with F. Barnaby) *Arms Uncontrolled*; *The Origin of the Strategic Cruise Missile*; and *The Road to War on Iraq*.

Lu Dehong is deputy director of the research department at the China Foundation for International and Strategic Studies. His main research areas include defence policy and strategic planning. He received his PhD from the National Defense University, PLA. Before demobilisation from the army, he served as staff officer in the China Ministry of National Defense.

Pan Guang is the director and professor of the Shanghai Center for International Studies and Institute of European & Asian Studies at the Shanghai Academy of Social Sciences, director of the SCO (Shanghai Cooperation Organisation) Studies Center in Shanghai, dean of the Center of Jewish Studies Shanghai (CJSS) and vice chairman of Chinese Society of Middle East Studies. He is also the International Council Member of Asia Society in USA, Senior Advisor of the China-Eurasia Forum in USA, an advisory board member of the *Asia Europe Journal* (by ASEF) in Singapore and senior advisor on anti-terror affairs to the Shanghai Municipality and Ministry of Public Security of PRC. His awards include the James Friend Annual Memorial Award for Sino-Jewish Studies (1993), the Special Award for Research on Canadian Jews from China (1996), and the Sankt Peterburg-300 Medal for Contribution to China-Russia Relations, which was awarded in 2004 by then Russia President Vladimir Putin. In 2006 he received the Austria Holocaust Memorial Award. In 2005 he was nominated by then UN Secretary-General Kofi Annan to be a member of the High-Level Group for the UN Alliance of Civilizations. He has undertaken research and lectured widely in North America, East Asia, Russia, Centre Asia, Europe, the Middle East and Australia. He has published such works as *The Jews in China* and *From Silk Road to Asem: 2000 Years of Asia-Europe Relations*. Other topics include the 2003 US War on Iraq, relations between China, Central Asia, and Russia; SCO and China's role in the war on terrorism; contemporary international crises; China's success in the Middle East; the anti-terrorism strategy and the role in the war on terror of China; Islam and Confucianism and the development of Islam in China; ethnic and religious conflicts in the Pacific Rim area; and China and post-Soviet Central Asia.

Brendan Taylor is a lecturer in the Graduate Studies in Strategy and Defence program at the Strategic Defence Studies Centre, The Australian National University. Dr Taylor is the course coordinator for the program elective 'The US and East Asian Security'. His research interests include Northeast Asian security, American foreign policy, economic statecraft, and alliance politics. He lectures to a number of undergraduate and postgraduate classes at The Australian National University—where he coordinates Masters-level courses on 'Asia-Pacific security' and 'The US and East Asian security'—as well as to various Australian Defence Colleges and public fora. He is a member of the Australian Committee of the Council for Security Cooperation in the Asia-Pacific. His publications have appeared in such leading international journals as *Asian Security*, *Comparative Strategy*, and the *Australian Journal of International Affairs*. He also co-authored (with D. Ball and A. Milner) *Mapping Track II Institutions in New Zealand, Australia and the Asian Region, An Independent Study Submitted to the Asia New Zealand Foundation in March 2005*.

Yuan Peng is currently director of the Institute of American Studies, China Institutes of Contemporary International Relations (CICIR). His research focuses on US foreign policy, China-US relations, cross-Strait relations, and East Asian-Pacific Security Studies. He served as a senior fellow of the CNAPS Program (Center for Northeast Asian Policy Studies) at the Brookings Institution from September 2003 to June 2004, and visiting scholar in the Senior Fellow Program at the Atlantic Council of the United States form December 1999 to June 2000. His latest books are *American Think-Tanks and Their Attitudes Towards China* (editor-in-chief, 2003) and *China-U.S. Relations: A Strategic Analysis* (co-editor, 2005). He has also published articles in Chinese newspapers such as *People's Daily*, *China Daily*, and *Global Times*.

Zhai Kun is the director of Southeast Asian and the Oceanian Studies of China Institutes of Contemporary International Relations. His areas of expertise include

Southeast Asia, Oceania, East Asian cooperation and Asia-Europe cooperation. In addition to his academic pursuits, Zhai Kun is a columnist and an adviser to China Central Television.

Zhang Tuosheng is a senior fellow, chairman of the academic assessment committee, and director of the Department of Research at the China Foundation for International and Strategic Studies. During the early 1990s, he served as the deputy defence attaché at the Chinese embassy in the United Kingdom. His main research interests are Sino-US relations, Sino-Japan relations, Asia-Pacific security, and Chinese foreign policy.

Zhu Feng is a professor in the School of International Studies and director of the International Security Program at Peking University. He is a leading Chinese security expert and senior research fellow of the Center for Peace and Development of China. He writes extensively on international security in East Asia, power relations and China-US-Japan security ties.

Acronyms and Abbreviations

APEC	Asia-Pacific Economic Cooperation
APT	ASEAN Plus Three
ARC	Australian Research Council
ARF	ASEAN Regional Forum
ASEAN	Association of Southeast Asian Nations
CCPCC	Chinese Communist Party's Central Committee
CFISS	China Foundation for International and Strategic Studies
CSCAP	Council for Security Cooperation in the Asia-Pacific
EAS	East Asia Summit
FTA	Free Trade Agreement
NATO	North Atlantic Treaty Organization
NDP	National Defense Panel
NGO	Non-governmental organisation
PLA	People's Liberation Army
PSI	Proliferation Security Initiative
QDR	*Quadrennial Defense Review*
RATS	Regional Anti-Terrorist Structure
SARS	Severe Acute Respiratory Syndrome
SCO	Shanghai Cooperation Organisation
SDSC	Strategic and Defence Studies Centre
TAC	*Treaty of Amity and Cooperation*
TSD	Trilateral Strategic Dialogue
2MRC	two medium regional conflicts
UNSC	United Nations Security Council
WMD	Weapons of Mass Destruction
WTO	World Trade Organization

List of Tables

Table 1	China's Imports from North Korea from January–July 2005 to January–July 2006 ($ in US millions)	55
Table 2	China's Exports to North Korea from January–July 2005 to January–July 2006 ($ in US millions)	55

Chapter 1

Introduction

Ron Huisken

The papers in this monograph were prepared for a workshop organised by the Strategic and Defence Studies Centre (SDSC) in partnership with the China Foundation for International and Strategic Studies (CFISS), and held in Beijing in March 2007. The workshop and, indeed, the establishment of the partnership with the CFISS was made possible by an ARC Linkage Grant (with the Department of Defence as the 'Industry Partner') awarded to the SDSC in 2005. The ARC grant has made it possible for the SDSC to network more systematically with other centres of learning in the Asia-Pacific focused on the strategic ramifications of China's rise. It has enabled the Centre to offer additional courses on China in its Masters program and, more generally, to boost the Centre's interest and capacity to conduct research on issues related to China. The Centre is indebted to both the ARC and the Department of Defence for this support.

The workshop was attended, on the Australian side, by all three 'Chief Investigators' for the ARC-funded project, namely Ron Huisken, Robert Ayson, and Brendan Taylor. As this was the inaugural collaboration with the CFISS, Yu Ping, the then Administrator of the Masters program and a Chinese citizen, participated as our liaison officer, adding valuable ballast to the Australian team. For its part, the CFISS assembled its director and deputy director of research, Zhang Tuosheng and Lu Dehong respectively, together with four other scholars from centres in Beijing and Shanghai: Pan Guang, Yuan Peng, Zhai Kun and Zhu Feng. Most of the Chinese papers were written in Chinese and translated into English. We elected, as far as possible, to preserve the flavour of these translations and limited our editing to the correction of any obvious sources of confusion or misinterpretation. It is appropriate to make clear at this point that the workshop participants are responsible only for the content of their papers. Responsibility for these introductory observations rests solely with the editor.

The theme for the workshop, suggested by the SDSC, was *Developing East Asia's Security Architecture*. The broad intent was to get behind the Chinese view that the extant architecture, dominated of course by America's several bilateral alliance relationships, reflects a Cold War mentality that should now give way to thinking better suited to the challenges and opportunities of the contemporary world. China's official alternative is encapsulated in the slogans for a revival of multipolarity and the democratisation of international relations, and in its New Security Concept which urges adherence to principles like mutual benefit and mutual respect. We wondered whether China's academic community might be toying with ideas that could operationalise this general dissatisfaction with the status quo.

Not surprisingly, perhaps, the workshop papers only came at this issue tangentially. Dissatisfaction with the status quo was strongly confirmed but, beyond an unmistakable preference to see a gradual diminution in US prominence, no concepts for an alternative regional architecture were hinted at. Both the papers and the discussions at the workshop, apart from proving to be a rich source of insights on specific issues, also confirmed that China has stepped away from any direct challenge to existing arrangements in favour of indirect and longer-term stratagems. Readers will be able to judge for themselves the degree of progress that China has made, but this observer's assessment would be in the ballpark of 'strong progress'.

One of the more interesting outcomes from the workshop actually came before it got underway. In March 2007, Australia had just signed the declaration with Japan on cooperation in the security field and our Chinese hosts were eager to hear what we had to say about it. Our attempts at an explanation—that it was a declaration not a treaty, that all of the activities envisaged were at the 'soft end' of the security spectrum, and that it was an incremental step in a relationship that had matured slowly but steadily over several decades—seemed to fall short of the mark. The light-hearted observation was made that China had clearly misread Australia in that the move toward Japan indicated that Australia had already decided which camp it preferred. This comment not only confirmed that Japan remains something of a raw nerve for China, but also that at least some Chinese scholars are already thinking instinctively in terms of rival 'camps' in East Asia, with China at the head of one of them. It also raised the question (but no opportunity presented itself to explore the answer) of why the specialist community in China (or parts of it) had come to the conclusion that Australia could be categorised as wavering between the 'alternative camps' in East Asia. Further discussion reverted to more familiar expressions of understanding for Australia's closeness to the United States (and, by extension, Japan), but included the speculation that Beijing might well seek to get closer to Australia to dilute any effort to forge an anti-China coalition.

The first theme tackled at the workshop was an evaluation of existing multilateral processes, particularly those associated with the Association of Southeast Asian Nations (ASEAN). In chapter 2 Brendan Taylor presents a crisp assessment of how regard for multilateral processes started hesitantly from a low base in the aftermath of the Cold War and then literally blossomed from the late 1990s, arguably to the point of oversupply. Taylor also tackles the tricky question of effectiveness, concluding that, against yardsticks such as networking, socialisation and confidence-building, the processes in East Asia deserve strong marks. At the same time, none of these processes have displayed much potential to deliver prompt, practical outcomes in crises and emergencies in the region like East Timor in 1999, the Severe Acute Respiratory Syndrome (SARS) outbreak in 2003 or the 26 December 2004 Indian Ocean Tsunami. These considerations feed into Taylor's judgement that in order to be part of a viable architecture for regional security, multilateral processes need to become more responsive to great power politics.

This sentiment dovetails rather nicely with Zhai Kun's creative endeavour to account for the most conspicuous dimension of multilateralism in East Asia, namely the dominance of ASEAN rather than one or more of the major powers. In chapter 3 Zhai contends that ASEAN's success is linked to redefining such notions as power and security to its advantage, and to its recognition that its ability to continue to shape the manner in which the great powers engage Southeast Asia is strongly linked to the deepening of ASEAN cohesion so that this grouping continues to be the standard-setter in the region on this front. The general idea is that ASEAN leadership of these processes must continue to look to all the major powers as better than the more costly and riskier approach of direct competition among them. Zhai further contends that China's decision to give unequivocal backing to ASEAN's aspirations to play this role has provided both essential strategic support and encouraged the other great powers to play the game ASEAN's way. This is an intriguing thesis. China has certainly achieved a significant status within ASEAN in a remarkably short space of time, despite the earlier dominance of Japan and, to some extent, at one remove, of the United States. Equally, however, if the brawl over the shape and role of the East Asia Summit (EAS) is any guide, great power competition is suspended only to the extent that it suits those powers.

In chapter 4, also covering East Asia's current multilateral processes, Pan Guang addresses the Shanghai Cooperation Organisation (SCO), which emerged in 1996 but took its present shape in 2001. Pan records the remarkable development of this China-initiated multilateral forum, including the plausible claim to have outflanked the United States despite the latter's dramatic intrusion into central Asia from October 2001 to prosecute the war against terrorism. In contrast to its caution in the ASEAN Regional Forum (ARF) during the 1990s, China has fast-tracked the development of the SCO, both in terms of the organisation's mandate and in giving the body concrete institutional form. The SCO's mandate has grown beyond its original purpose of defining and stabilising China's borders with Russia and the adjacent republics of the former Soviet Union, branching out into collaboration on counter-terrorism and seeking to be influential in shaping the development and distribution of the region's energy resources. Pan points out that stabilising some 15 000 km of land borders in Asia constitutes a major contribution of regional security. Similarly, he argues that the SCO's counter-terrorism campaign is of strategic significance for the whole of Asia, not least because the terrorist groups in Southeast Asia (which are potentially capable of disrupting energy supplies throughout the Indonesian archipelago) have close ties with the groups in central and south Asia. Although pre-eminently a security body, Pan Guang points out that the SCO's success on this front will also require a conscious effort to ensure an adequate degree of balanced economic development amongst all the participants.

In discussions on this paper, it was acknowledged that there seemed to be, at best, limited compatibility between Chinese and US interests in central Asia. Chinese participants repeatedly highlighted China's vulnerability to instability in Afghanistan and expressed genuine concern that the combined efforts of the United States and the North Atlantic Treaty Organization (NATO) in that country appeared to be inadequate. There was no suggestion, however, that China might, or should, consider a substantive military contribution to this campaign (although it was acknowledged that the United States has pressed for such a commitment on more than one occasion).

The two presentations on the Six-Party Talks process produced an enlightening discussion. China's protestations early in these negotiations—that its access and influence in North Korea had limits—tended to be regarded as 'cover' for a degree of common ground between Beijing and Pyongyang. This apparent consensus extended to how the nuclear crisis should be resolved, particularly as regards the timeframe, and how strongly the regime in Pyongyang should resist pressures on it to begin to change the nature of its governance of North Korea. The workshop discussions provided a timely reminder that if Japan and the United States have been North Korea's principal enemies over the past 60 years, for the preceding 2000 years or longer that position had belonged to China. It was pointed out that the close China-North Korea relationship of earlier times—rather famously likened to 'lips and teeth'—was borne of an era when China felt threatened and was seeking additional means, not least buffer states between itself and US forces, to bolster its security. Now it is North Korea that feels threatened and insecure, not least, perhaps, because both the Soviet Union/Russia and China distanced themselves from Pyongyang in the early 1990s.

In chapter 5, Zhu Feng provides a frank and fascinating assessment of the dynamics of the Beijing-Pyongyang relationship in recent years, and of Beijing's eventual conclusion that it may have seriously misread Pyongyang's motives and intentions. Zhu concludes that, following the missile tests of July 2006 and the nuclear test of October 2006, Beijing may well have concluded that it had little choice but to make clear to Pyongyang that it too regarded all options as being on the table if it reneged on its repeated assurances that it sought arrangements which would allow it to roll back its nuclear weapons program.

Introduction

In chapter 6, Robert Ayson takes an entirely different approach with his opening observation that the Six-Party Talks process is unlikely to result in the complete elimination of North Korea's nuclear weapons program. For Ayson, failure on this front does not mean that the Six-Party Talks process is without merit. To the contrary, he argues that there is a dimension to these talks that could more than offset a failure to fully achieve their declared purpose. For Ayson, the Six-Party Talks provide the one forum in which the region's three great powers—the United States, China and Japan—are being required to adapt and reconcile their approaches to an urgent regional security issue; that is, to develop the habits, instincts, and techniques of functioning as a 'concert of powers'. This positions the Six-Party Talks as the most promising countervailing force to those other tendencies at work in the region that point to the more dangerous option of rival blocs.

In the discussion in chapters 5 and 6, it is suggested that South Korea and North Korea are pursuing similar strategies for the longer term—more balanced relationships with their powerful neighbours, protectors and protagonists. For South Korea, this means enhancing its exposure to China and accepting some greater distance from the United States; while, for North Korea, it means measured engagement with the United States and Japan so as to lessen its exposure to China. This is a plausible line of argument and casts new light on the twists and turns of the Six-Party Talks. It is further supported by intense speculation within the think-tank community in Beijing (that the author encountered in October 2007) to the effect that the United States and North Korea had come to an understanding that has yet to be shared with the other Six-Party players. This speculation centres on a meeting in Berlin in May 2007 involving (then) US Secretary of State Condoleezza Rice, Assistant Secretary of State for East Asian and Pacific Affairs Christopher Hill and the chief North Korean negotiator to the Six-Party Talks.

These additional facets on the Six-Party Talks suggest that the longer-term endeavour to build a robustly stable security environment in Northeast Asia will be a challenging but fascinating exercise, and that expectations that South Korea and North Korea, whether separately or re-united, must inevitably slip wholesale into China's sphere of influence might be misplaced. Chinese participants in the workshop confirmed other indications that Beijing is favourably disposed to seeing the Six-Party Talks process transition into a standing security mechanism for the region. Since the United States is also of this view, the outlook for such a development must be deemed to be quite positive provided, of course, that the Six-Party Talks process can achieve the disablement of North Korea's nuclear weapons program in a manner that builds confidence in North Korea's intentions.

One of the themes strongly re-affirmed at the workshop was that China, alongside acknowledging that the United States was vastly and comprehensively more powerful, appears to be entirely comfortable with the notion of being a 'peer competitor'. It seems to be regarded as almost axiomatic (and, it must said, not without justification) that China will, in due course, become the second player in America's league in terms of a pronounced margin of superiority over all other states in economic weight, political clout, and military power. This self-image, as effectively the sole challenger to the present unipolar structure of the international system, naturally inclines some Chinese analysts to view the United States as by far the most formidable challenge to the full flourishing of China's potential. This also suggests, however, that China-US relations, for all the tranquility of recent years, are prone to be characterised by deep and powerful competitive instincts, and have a strong inherent potential to become strategically unstable.

In chapter 7, Ron Huisken provides an essentially familiar 'Western' account of US interests in and aspirations for East Asia, but is a good deal more cautious on the potential for the United States and China to achieve some form of strategic accommodation over the near to medium term than Lu Dehong expresses in chapter 8. Huisken's analysis supports a view expressed in workshop discussions that even if Washington gradually concedes that it must compromise on its status as the unambiguous foremost power globally, in Europe or in the Middle East, it will be most resistant to relinquishing its status in Asia. This view has inherent plausibility insofar as the synergies that in the past attached to pre-eminence in Europe and the Middle East will be more strongly attached to East Asia in the future simply because 'the most important bilateral relationship in the world in this century' (to borrow Hillary Clinton's words) is that between the United States and China.

In chapter 8, Lu Dehong, a retired People's Liberation Army (PLA) officer, presents his understanding (based on a careful study of critical and mostly left-of-centre American literature) of the complex and somewhat dysfunctional manner in which the United States goes about the business of protecting and advancing its interests. Lu contrasts this with the clarity and simplicity of pronouncements from China's leaders regarding security and defence policy. He concludes with an eloquent plea for an early and comprehensive program of strategic engagement between China and the United States in the conviction that this can expose the essential compatibility of their interests and aspirations.

In chapter 9, Yuan Peng seeks to back up the proposition that the prevailing stability in US-China relations is tactical rather than strategic. In doing so, he detects a degree of focus and coherence, and of danger, in US dealings with China that few Western analysts would relate to, but which dramatises a distinctive feature of international relations: just how differently a common set of events and developments can be perceived by various players.

The workshop took place just as Tokyo and Beijing made a serious effort to break and melt the ice that had encrusted China-Japan relations since the mid-1990s. Accordingly, the concluding presentation at the workshop was Zhang Tuosheng's account of why and how this effort was engineered and his assessment of the outlook for this central relationship. In chapter 10 Zhang points out that this core relationship deteriorated over the years up to 2006—to the point where it caused serious damage to the strategic interests of both sides, including the unbalancing of the US–China–Japan triangle. He contends that the more conspicuous sources of tension—the history issue, Taiwan, and the territorial disputes in the East China Sea—played out against the background of a deeper concern: the end of the Cold War exposed the unsettling reality of two major powers in East Asia. Zhang's qualified optimism about the quite comprehensive revival of political engagement since (then) Japanese Prime Minister Shinzo Abe's visit to Beijing in October 2006, including China's acceptance in a joint communiqué in April 2007 of a bigger Japanese role in international affairs, was tested in the discussions that followed his presentation. This discussion only confirmed the veracity of Zhang's concluding observation that, absent a genuine reconciliation between China and Japan, any architecture of security in East Asia will look worryingly inadequate.

A familiar approach to assessing the reliability of a region's 'security architecture' is to weigh the strength of potential challenges to security and stability against the authority of the institutions, mechanisms and processes available to develop instincts to accommodate national preferences to the collective interests of regional states, to resolve instances of conflicting aspirations, and to deter any inclinations to use national power to intimidate or coerce others into line in a manner that falls outside accepted norms of diplomatic interaction between states. This architecture is typically seen as composed of three elements: bilateral relationships, alliances, and multilateral institutions and processes. Commonsense (and scientific principles) allows the inference that the most robust architectural form is one that incorporates all three elements and where all the elements are of equal weight and importance. Of course, scientific principles are rather difficult to replicate in any structure involving people. And there is a school of thought that, in this example, two elements are in fact better than three, because the third, alliances, is by its very nature 'us versus them' institutions and inherently incompatible with the inculcation of comprehensive, collective and common security mindsets. Equally, it is not very difficult to develop a compelling argument that alliances are an indispensable 'contradiction' on the road to the adoption of genuine and reliable collective or collegiate approaches to security.

In East Asia at the end of the Cold War, such a security tripod could be detected, but its legs were conspicuously uneven in that the multilateral leg was all but invisible. Over the past 15 years, all three legs of the tripod have experienced considerable change. The mosaic of bilateral relationships has generally become thicker and stronger, with the China-Japan relationship being the most conspicuous exception. Alliance relationships have also been dynamic, becoming arguably more distant in the case of the US-South Korea relationship and closer and more comprehensive in the case of the US-Japan relationship. But the arena of most conspicuous change has been the development of multilateral processes. From essentially none, we now have ASEAN Plus Ten, the Asia-Pacific Economic Cooperation (APEC), the ARF, the SCO, ASEAN Plus Three (APT), and the EAS, with expectations that the Six-Party Talks will spawn a new, standing mechanism. But the question, of course, is whether all these acronyms add up to a tripod leg of equal strength; that is, that it makes a contribution to regional security that is commensurate with the other two. I would venture the view that this is not the case; that there is, in fact, a nagging sense that States in the region have danced around the issue of building a multilateral process based on an acceptance that all the major powers now embedded in the region have a full role to play in shaping its future.

The prominent role that ASEAN has played on the multilateral front is, in part, a reflection of the continuing ambivalence among the major powers on who should be accepted as a key sculptor of the region's security architecture and on the character of the institution in which this artistic function should be performed. ASEAN's claim to leadership of the process rests on the assurance that it will be a 'safe driver, proceeding at a pace comfortable to all'. Among other things, this means gauging major power interests and not testing the limits of their tolerance. If ASEAN misjudges, or if an initiative runs outside expected parameters, the major powers will normally make clear that a policy correction is in order. Something of this kind appears to have occurred, with the EAS holdings its first session with India, Australia and New Zealand as founding members and Russia all but promised early admission. China was prepared to shed its benevolent image and require ASEAN to belittle this new body by stressing that the real engine-room for community-building in East Asia would remain the narrower APT forum. The ASEAN processes have by no means been ineffective, but they are an indirect and therefore slow-acting way forward. In the meantime, a significant and possibly growing amount of major power energy is being channelled into multilateral processes that exclude perceived rivals and which are directly or indirectly competitive with existing processes set up by these rivals.

We cannot expect in East Asia over the foreseeable future to see the sort of pooling of sovereignty that has occurred in Europe. We must anticipate that, for the foreseeable future, the requirement will be for the sensible management and containment of competitive instincts. The establishment of a multilateral security body in East Asia that includes all the key players, and which the major powers invest with the authority to tackle the shaping of the regional security order, remains a critical piece of unfinished business.

Chapter 2

Developing East Asia's Security Architecture: An Australian perspective on ASEAN processes

Brendan Taylor

Prior to the 1990s, a tangible East Asian security architecture remained elusive. This was not for want of trying. Several ill-fated efforts were undertaken to establish regional groupings which, over time, provided the basis for a more substantial East Asian security architecture. These included the Southeast Asia Treaty Organisation (SEATO)—an eight member grouping established in 1955 that began to lose members and was finally dissolved in 1977, and both Maphilindo and the Association of Southeast Asia (ASA).[1] Likewise, in Northeast Asia, the Asian and Pacific Council (ASPAC)—a South Korean initiative established in 1966 and comprising nine member countries—struggled due to the diverging perceptions and interests of its membership, and finally collapsed in 1975.[2] Flowing from this legacy was the more successful sub-regional Association of Southeast Asian Nations (ASEAN), founded in 1967 and expanded via several avenues, including a major security component, the ASEAN Regional Forum (ARF). But even ASEAN's initial collaborative functions were essentially economic, political and cultural.

This paucity in regional security dialogue stands in stark contrast to the situation today where, according to one recent estimate, over 100 such channels now exist at the official (Track 1) level and in excess of 200 at the unofficial (Track 2) level.[3] To be sure, this startling growth in regional security cooperation has been neither steady nor straightforward. The volume of such institutions and activities plummeted in the immediate aftermath of the 1997–98 Asian financial crisis, for instance, and temporarily lost the attention of policymakers in the process. Yet there can be little disputing the fact that regional security cooperation has since recovered well and, moreover, that the general trend in such activity across the decade and a half since the beginning of the 1990s has been an upward one. ASEAN, of course, has been one of the key drivers or 'architects' behind this trend. This chapter evaluates the effectiveness and the shortcomings of the most prominent ASEAN processes. It considers the outlook for these, before concluding with an Australian perspective on their desirable future development.

Evaluating ASEAN processes

Before reflecting upon the effectiveness and shortcomings of ASEAN processes, it is necessary to firstly acknowledge that this evaluative task is an inevitably subjective one. As Amitav Acharya has observed:

> Despite decades of intense debate, international relations theory provides no agreed and definitive way of assessing what constitutes 'success' and 'effectiveness' in regional organizations. Understanding the effects of Asian institutions on state behavior and regional order depends very much on the analytical lens used.[4]

By way of example, many if not most regional players will tend to assess regional security cooperation not in terms of its immediate *outcomes*, but rather as a *process* through which confidence is built, consensus reached and common regional understandings or 'norms' arrived at.

This issue of analytical subjectivity notwithstanding, it is, I think, possible to identify a number of areas where ASEAN processes have unequivocally fallen short. None of these processes, for instance, has proven able to respond effectively to the major crises that have erupted in East Asia during the past decade and a half—the North Korean nuclear crises of 1993–94 and today; the 1995–96 Taiwan Strait crisis; the 1997–98 Asian financial crisis; the crisis in East Timor of 1999; the 2003 Severe Acute Respiratory Syndrome (SARS) crisis or the 26 December 2004 Indian Ocean Tsunami. Partly as a result of the consensual style approach to decision-making which has emerged as the preferred modus operandi for most if not all of these processes, they have also tended to move rather slowly toward implementing their stated aims and objectives. In the case of the ARF, for instance, it has experienced real difficulties in moving from the confidence-building to preventive diplomacy phase in its evolution, contributing toward the perception that it is nothing more than a 'talk shop'.[5]

These criticisms notwithstanding—and even if one does not accept the proposition that dialogue and discussion are useful as ends in and of themselves[6] —there are areas where tangible benefits have accrued from the recent growth in East Asian security cooperation. First and foremost among these accomplishments, in my view, has been the engagement of China in the regional security architecture which has taken place since the mid-1990s. This process has succeeded in significantly dampening regional apprehensions regarding China's rise. At the same time, however, it is interesting to note that while a primary aim of engaging China through East Asian security cooperation was to 'socialise' it by exposing it to regional and global norms, Beijing has proven rather adept at 'socialising' many of the institutions to which it is a party. By way of example, in the case of the Council for Security Cooperation in the Asia-Pacific (CSCAP)—the official Track 2 analogue of the ARF—China's deepening involvement has actually allowed it to shape the direction and outlook of this leading Track 2 institution, particularly in relation to the issue of Taiwan.

Further, although ASEAN processes have been somewhat ineffective in responding directly to regional crises, they have periodically served as useful venues for the discussion of highly sensitive or controversial issues that might otherwise not have been discussed, or as 'circuit-breakers' to stalled diplomatic relationships. The then US Secretary of State, Colin Powell, was able to meet with his North Korean counterpart on the sidelines of the 2004 ARF meeting, for example, which marked the first high-level contact between the United States and North Korea since former US Secretary of State Madeleine Albright's visit to Pyongyang in 2000. More recently, the Chinese and Japanese foreign ministers held a productive 20-minute meeting on the sidelines of the 2006 ARF, helping to alleviate somewhat a deepening rift in China-Japan relations. So, in sum, it seems fair to conclude that ASEAN processes have served as more than mere 'talks shops' and that they have produced some tangible successes, albeit highly qualified ones and often only at the margins.

Added to this, the very existence and continued evolution of ASEAN can itself be counted as a success. It is always important to consider counterfactual scenarios in international politics, and to contemplate what type of Southeast Asia might exist today were it not for the existence of ASEAN. It is certainly no small feat that a 'shooting war' amongst its members is today all but unthinkable. As Rodolfo Severino of the Singapore-based Institute of Southeast Asian Studies (ISEAS) recently put it:

> The constant interaction and sense of common purpose among the Asean members have built mutual confidence and dissipated some of the mutual suspicion that is a legacy of past differences and an outgrowth of current disagreements. ... Partly through the Treaty of Amity and Cooperation in South-east Asia and partly through its own practices, Asean has set regional norms for the peaceful relations among states—respect for sovereignty and territorial integrity, the peaceful settlement of disputes, non-interference in the internal affairs of nations, decisions by consensus, equality of status, and so on.[7]

Where to from here?

So having canvassed the effectiveness and shortcomings of ASEAN processes, what is the future outlook for these mechanisms? The answer to this question will, in my view, be determined by the influence of at least three key factors.

First, the rapidly changing dynamics of the East Asian strategic environment will profoundly shape the future activities and, indeed, viability of ASEAN processes. Security threats and challenges will influence the demand for regional security cooperation but, just as importantly, the strategic environment itself will also largely determine the areas in which progress is most and least viable. Non-traditional security issues such as infectious disease, terrorism, transnational crime, and disaster prevention/mitigation will be increasingly critical. In May 2006, for example, the inaugural ASEAN Defence Ministers meeting in Kuala Lumpur, Malaysia, identified disaster relief cooperation as a priority issue upon which to focus its future work. Likewise, as part of its transition from confidence-building to practical cooperation, the ARF has been asked to adopt collaborative measures for addressing non-traditional security challenges, if only to demonstrate its continuing relevance in an increasingly crowded East Asian security architecture.[8] Addressing these kinds of trans-border challenges is needed not only because they are becoming increasingly pressing and potentially affect the region as a whole, but also because they will often tend not to raise the same level of sensitivity (particularly in relation to such strongly partisan issues as sovereignty and non-intervention) as that generated by more traditional security issues.

Second, the sheer volume of regional institutions and the growing number of aspiring regional security 'architects' could well have significant implications for ASEAN processes. In a relatively short space of time, for instance, China has established itself as a leading regional architect. The United States has been slow to react, but also looks set to remain an influential player given its unprecedented military power and considerable economic weight in the region. India too has become an increasingly involved and accepted member of such leading mechanisms as the East Asia Summit (EAS). As India's economic and strategic weight continues to grow, its willingness and potential ability to further contribute towards influencing the shape and design of any East Asian security architecture will also increase in kind. The question remains, however, as to whether ASEAN can continue to exert the influence it has previously enjoyed in this increasingly crowded and competitive institutional environment. Moreover, questions also remain as to whether the associated upward trend in dialogue activity is even going to be sustainable over the longer term. To employ an analogy with which interdependence theorists in international relations would be well acquainted, is there potential for the East Asian security architecture to fall victim to an over-abundance of such institutions leading to the demise of a number of them?[9] In other words, can there be such a thing as too much security interaction among the countries of any given region which yields greater density but insufficient commonality? If so, how much is too much and what are the policy implications of this?

Third, ASEAN processes will ultimately remain hostage to the fact that state-centric factors related to both interests and values will need to be faced and resolved if a successful security architecture is to be achieved in East Asia.

In this context, great power politics will arguably remain the most crucial determinant, and the future of the US-China relationship will be especially pivotal. Would the United States have been excluded from the EAS, for instance, and would Washington's recent (re)engagement with regional fora such as the ARF have occurred were the United States and China not potential strategic rivals? Likewise, the future of the China-Japan relationship will be critical in defining East Asian security architecture, as the inaugural EAS demonstrated all too vividly. How such rivalries can be modified or finessed sufficiently to cultivate a longer-term sense of 'community'—the tacit but widely understood vision underlying the need for a successful security architecture in this region—is not yet clear. Still, it is reasonable to conclude that such success will remain elusive if more traditional norms or means of securing state-centric interests triumph. The most basic challenge posited by the concept of 'security architecture' is how much its alleged proponents genuinely wish to fulfil this vision and to work collectively to overcome the challenges embodied in realising it.

Desirable future development—An Australian perspective

Aside from a complete collapse of the East Asian security order (brought about, for example, by a catastrophic breakdown in China-US or China-Japan relations), the 'nightmare scenario' for Australia in the face of these developments is that it could become marginalised altogether from the region, or at least from its more influential and important institutions. The most likely avenue through which this could happen would be Australia's exclusion from organisations built on a burgeoning 'East Asian' identity. Australia's participation in the 2004 ASEAN Plus Three (APT) meeting and its membership of the EAS have gone some way toward assuaging these fears. That said, Australia is far from being a key player in either of these mechanisms. Residual apprehensions remain, with the jury still out on how far these emergent processes will go in advancing the potentially powerful notion of an East Asian Community.

It is important to bear in mind here that, at least in its relations with the East Asian region, Australia sees itself as a deeply vulnerable and insecure nation. In his classic 1979 book *The frightened country*, the former head of the Australian Department of Foreign Affairs, Alan Renouf, describes Australia as a country that literally lives in fear of its own neighbourhood. It is therefore, in Renouf's view, a country that is unable to see the opportunities in the Asian region clearly and one that also exhibits a strong penchant for seeking out a 'great and powerful friend' to compensate for its perceived strategic insecurities.[10] First it was Britain in the period up until the Second World War; then the United States through the post-war period and up until the present day. Further complicating this innate sense of insecurity, the late Harvard political scientist Samuel Huntington has described Australia as a 'torn country', a society divided over whether or not it belongs to Asia.[11] In his terms

> the lucky country will be a permanently torn country, both the 'branch office of empire', which [the former Australian Prime Minister] Paul Keating decried, and the 'new white trash of Asia', which Lee Kuan Yew contemptuously termed it.[12]

Through its favoured 'exclusivist' approach towards East Asian security architecture, China has inadvertently reinforced Australia's sense of isolation and vulnerability. This was most evident in the run up to the inaugural EAS, when Beijing reportedly preferred a gathering limited to APT members and did not actively support Australia's attendance.[13] Similar concern has been expressed in relation to the Shanghai Cooperation Organisation (SCO), which also excludes Australia, but whose members and observers represent half of the world's population. Antipodean anxiety is even mirrored at the Track 2 level, where recent initiatives such as the Network of East Asian Think Tanks (NEAT) are regarded by some as a (Chinese-led) challenge to more established processes in which Australia is already a key player, such as CSCAP.[14]

Canberra has responded to these dilemmas by continuing to engage with those processes through which the powerful idea of a distinctly East Asian Community appears most likely to materialise—namely APT and the EAS—even while conceding that Australia is unlikely to become a particularly influential or integral member of such groupings. At the same time, however, Canberra has indirectly balanced against the prospect of a more exclusive East Asian Community by throwing its weight behind competing mechanisms that exhibit a more inclusive communal ethos. Less than two months before the inaugural EAS in December 2005 (and against the backdrop of Australian euphoria at having been included in this fledgling mechanism), the then Australian Prime Minister, John Howard, described APEC as 'undeniably the most important international meeting with which Australia is associated'.[15] Subsequently, Howard pledged his support to a Japanese initiative to establish a free trade zone comprising of 16 Asia-Pacific nations.[16] Simultaneously, Australia has supported initiatives comprising of those countries traditionally regarded as regional 'outsiders'—namely the United States, Japan and India—who potentially have the most to lose from any realisation of the East Asian Community ideal. Australian support for US-led multilateral mechanisms with a regional focus, such as the controversial Proliferation Security Initiative (PSI) and the Ministerial-level Trilateral Strategic Dialogue (TSD) involving the United States, Japan, Australia (and potentially India), could be interpreted as a form of indirect balancing or 'insurance' against the prospect of its institutional marginalisation from the region. Indeed, so too can the March 2007 Australian security agreement with Japan.[17]

From Beijing's perspective, however, such initiatives can easily be interpreted as reflecting Australian support for a US (and possibly Japanese)-led campaign to constrain, if not completely contain, China's burgeoning regional influence. To be fair, there is some basis to this perception, given the existence of a small, yet relatively influential, anti-China lobby within Australia.[18] By and large, however, it is important to recognise that Australian views of China, and specifically its (re)emergence, are generally very different from those held in the United States and Japan. Of the three, Canberra is clearly the most sanguine on this issue. For Australia, China's rise is seen as nothing short of an economic blessing. Canberra has come out consistently with statements such as that issued at the beginning of 2006 by the then Australian Ambassador to the United States, Dennis Richardson, suggesting that 'the question for Australia is not whether China's growth is innately good or bad; Australia made up its mind long ago that it was a good thing. China's growth is unambiguously good for Asia and the United States'.[19] In relation to the issue of China's growing military capabilities, senior Australian officials are on record as describing 'China's expanding military expenditure as a process of modernisation, not destabilisation'.[20] Even with regard to human rights issues, Howard publicly stated in July 2005 that the China-Australia relationship was 'mature enough' to ride through 'temporary arguments' in this area and that he remain[ed] 'unashamed' in developing Australia's relations with China.[21]

Yet perceptions often matter most in international politics. To an extent that has yet to be fully appreciated, the analysis contained in this section suggests that competing approaches to order-building in East Asia have the potential to create serious tensions in this blossoming China-Australia relationship. From Canberra's perspective, Beijing's apparent preference for a more exclusive regional architecture has exacerbated Australia's longstanding vulnerability—to borrow from a former Australian Prime Minister, Paul Keating,—as 'the odd man out' in Asia.[22] For Beijing, equally, the strategy that Canberra has adopted to 'insure' against its possible regional marginalisation has been (mis)construed as signifying support for a containment of China that would ultimately not be in Australia's best interests. In the final analysis, therefore, because of the potential threat they pose to China-Australia ties, finding ways to allay these concerns will constitute an important task for the future sustainability of the Australia-China bilateral relationship more generally.

So what can be done? For Australia, greater attention clearly needs to be given to the 'packaging' or presentational aspects of its indirect balancing approach. The diplomacy surrounding the March 2007 announcement of the Australia-Japan security declaration and suggestions by Howard that this arrangement might evolve into a formal security treaty appear to have been largely targeted at an Australian domestic audience. Yet this is certainly not how they were read in Beijing. Greater transparency from Canberra in such instances would certainly not go amiss. Australia could also consider what scope there might be to lobby for the inclusion of China as an observer in some of the more exclusive arrangements to which Australia is a party, such as the TSD. Likewise, Beijing in return might be willing to consider some of the benefits of seeking Australian involvement in some of the more exclusive processes to which it is a party, working from the assumption that Canberra views a rising China very differently from Washington and Tokyo.

As Japan changes its international personality and seeks a greater degree of regional autonomy, and as ASEAN begins to question its own medium-to-longer term capacity to remain in the driver's seat of regional architecture-building, might there also be merit in developing a Trilateral Security (as opposed to Strategic) Dialogue between China, Japan and Australia? Despite the recent thawing which appears to be occurring in China-Japan ties—as epitomised by Chinese Premier Wen Jiabao's short but highly successful April 2007 visit to Tokyo—the extraordinarily deep societal and historical tensions between these two countries cannot be underestimated. Issues of energy security also appear inevitable to complicate the China-Japan relationship in the years ahead, while (as the two historical great powers of East Asia) both countries have much at stake—and potentially much over which to disagree—in seeking to refine and then implement the notion of an East Asian Community. Not least because China and Japan are Australia's leading trading partners, the prospect of spiraling tensions between them is of genuine concern to Canberra. To the extent that a new trilateral mechanism involving Beijing, Canberra and Tokyo could serve to avoid, alleviate or at the very least manage these tensions in the China-Japan relationship, it would be most welcome.

In theory at least, all of this should become more straightforward for Australia under the Rudd Government. Kevin Rudd is a mandarin speaker with a strong interest in China and in Asia-Pacific multilateralism. That said, the difficulties associated with executing a genuine and comprehensive process of China-Australia engagement should never be under-estimated. While the depth of Australia's economic engagement with China can hardly be called into question, its engagement at other levels remains relatively shallow and under-developed. Engagement, of course, is a multi-layered, multi-dimensional process that also encompasses a wide spectrum of people-to-people contacts and personal linkages. Yet, in many respects, Australia and China remain very different societies: we speak a different language, our cultures are diametrically opposed, and our values are often in conflict. Trying to develop the same level of trust and intimacy that currently exists in the Australia-US relationship is therefore likely to be a long-term project, and one that will almost certainly encounter a good deal more trials and tribulations than has thus far been acknowledged in either Beijing or Canberra. Developing a sounder understanding of our respective priorities and perceptions in the realm of Asia-Pacific multilateralism therefore represents a relatively innocuous yet important way to begin that process in earnest.

ENDNOTES

[1] John S. Duffield, 'Asia-Pacific Security Institutions in Comparative Perspective', in G. John Ikenberry and Michael Mastanduno (eds), *International Relations Theory and the Asia-Pacific*, Columbia University Press, New York, 2003, p. 248. Also see Charles E. Morrison and Astri Suhrke, *Strategies of Survival: the Foreign Policy Dilemmas of Smaller Asian States*, University of Queensland Press, St Lucia, 1978; and Leszek Buszynski, *SEATO, The Failure of an Alliance Strategy*, Singapore University Press, Singapore, 1983.

[2] See C.W. Braddick, 'Japan, Australia and the ASPAC: the rise and fall of an Asia-Pacific cooperative security framework', in Brad Williams and Andrew Newman (eds), *Japan, Australia and Asia-Pacific Security*, Routledge, London, 2006, pp. 30–46.

[3] See Japan Center for International Exchange, *Towards Community Building in East Asia, Dialogue and Research Monitor Overview Report, 2005*, available at <http://www.jcie.or.jp/drm>, accessed 5 May 2008.

[4] Amitav Acharya, 'Regional Institutions and Asian Security Order: Norms, Power, and Prospects for Peaceful Change', in Muthiah Alagappa (ed.), *Asian Security Order: Instrumental and Normative Features*, Stanford University Press, Stanford, 2003, p. 228.

[5] See, for example, Paul Dibb, 'A New Defence Policy for a New Strategic Era?', in Clive Williams and Brendan Taylor (eds), *Countering Terror: New Directions Post '911'*, Canberra Papers on Strategy and Defence no. 147, Strategic and Defence Studies Centre, The Australian National University, Canberra, 2003, p. 64.

[6] See, for example, Anthony Milner, *Region, Security and the Return of History*, Institute of Southeast Asian Studies, Singapore, 2003.

[7] Rodolfo C. Severino, 'Asean in need of stronger cohesion', *Straits Times*, 9 December 2006.

[8] Barry Desker, 'Is the ARF obsolete? Three steps to avoid irrelevance', *PacNet*, no. 37A, Pacific Forum CSIS, 27 July 2006.

[9] This point is raised by John Garofano, 'Power, Institutions and the ASEAN Regional Forum', *Asian Survey*, vol. 52, no. 3, May/June 2002, p. 506. The transmission belt problem has been discussed extensively by Robert Keohane and Joseph S. Nye, *Power and Interdependence*, 2nd edition, Little and Brown, Boston, 2002.

[10] Alan Renouf, *The frightened country*, MacMillan, Melbourne, 1979.

[11] Samuel P. Huntington, 'The Clash of Civilizations?', *Foreign Affairs*, vol. 72, no. 3, Summer 1993, p. 42.

[12] Samuel P. Huntington, *The Clash of Civilizations and the Remaking of World Order*, Simon & Schuster, New York, 1995, p. 153.

[13] See Patrick Walters, 'Beijing plays spoiler on Asia summit', *Australian*, 6 April 2005, p. 2.

[14] For further reading, see Brendan Taylor, Anthony Milner and Desmond Ball, *Track 2 Diplomacy in Asia: Australian and New Zealand Engagement*, Canberra Papers on Strategy and Defence no. 164, The Australian National University, Canberra, 2006, p. 68.

[15] Prime Minister the Hon. John Howard MP, 'Address to the APEC Australian Business Forum Dinner', Sheraton on the Park, Sydney, 21 October, 2005.

[16] Emma-Kate Symons, 'PM eyes regional trading bloc plan', *Australian*, 16 January 2007, p. 1.

[17] For further reading, see Brendan Taylor, 'The Australia-Japan Security Agreement: Between a Rock and a Hard Place?', *PacNet*, no 13, Pacific Forum, CSIS, Honolulu, 19 March 2007.

[18] See, for example, Paul Dibb, 'Don't get too close to Beijing', *Australian*, 2 August 2005, p. 12.

[19] Geoff Elliott, 'Stay cool on China, Ambassador tells US', *Australian*, 30 January 2006, p. 1.

[20] Cited in Dibb, 'Don't get too close to Beijing', *Australian*, 2 August 2005, p. 12.

[21] Transcript of the Prime Minister The Hon. John Howard MP, Joint Press Conference with The President of the United States of America George W. Bush, The White House, Washington, DC, 19 July 2005.

[22] Cited in Huntington, *The Clash of Civilizations and the Remaking of World Order*, p. 152.

Chapter 3

The ASEAN Power

Zhai Kun

It is taken for granted that the major countries have dominant status in the international community, while the minor ones have little influence. It is certainly assumed that they have more power than the minor countries. But this assumption often blinds us to the fact that small countries also seek to acquire and exploit power. In what kind of situations can such countries give the impression of playing on the same stage as the major powers? One answer is that they can acquire disproportionate power when they create a new kind of power resource and demonstrate that they can use this resource consistently to facilitate the emergence of a new world order.

This chapter analyses this contention by using the Association of Southeast Asian Nations (ASEAN) after the Cold War as a case study.

ASEAN power

ASEAN suffered the strike of the 1997–98 Asian financial crisis, and it experienced a low tide in the final years of the last century. But in the new century, along with the revival of the ASEAN member states' economies, ASEAN's regional status and function advanced incessantly. It has made great progress in the fields of its integration process, the East Asia cooperation process and the strategy of balance of powers, which have made the world view it with new eyes, with some scholars even contending that ASEAN is becoming the centre of power in East Asia.[1] There are four concrete representations of this burgeoning power.

First, ASEAN is changing the traditional cognition towards the ownership of power. As we still keep to the old idea that the Southeast Asia region is the arena where the big powers struggle to acquire a sphere of influence, ASEAN's strategy of balancing big powers has been in operation, with Singapore and Vietnam as the most conspicuous examples. The United States and Japan are 'jealous' that China's influence is increasing in the Southeast Asia region, so they constantly offer more 'carrots' to ASEAN member countries. For example, if a big power wants to join the East Asia Summit (EAS), a regional cooperation network created by ASEAN to avoid becoming a marginal player in the competition to shape community-building in the region, it has to achieve the qualifications set by ASEAN; for example, it has to join the *Treaty of Amity and Cooperation* (TAC). Because the United States is reluctant to join the TAC, it cannot become a member of the EAS.[2] Russia, on the other hand, has joined the TAC, but has also been refused entry into the EAS on the grounds that trade relations between the two sides remain relatively modest. ASEAN has achieved dominant status in the collective game with big powers.

Second, ASEAN is changing the traditional understanding about how countries seek to advance their interests. Generally speaking, the economic cooperation theory considers that when a large state and a small state are in the process of establishing a bilateral Free Trade Agreement (FTA), the larger one usually exerts its power to protect its economic interests, while the smaller one opens its market passively. The larger one becomes the axle country and gains more benefit by establishing FTAs with several small ones, which become the spoke countries and benefit less. For example, the United States intends to expand the North American Free Trade Agreement (NAFTA) to the whole American continent, and its aim is to realise its institutional hegemony in the American continent. While people still keep to the old idea of these countries seeking to protect and advance their interests, ASEAN actually bypassed the China-Japan nexus a decade ago, and created the East Asia cooperation framework including China, Japan and South Korea. These three nations recognise and support ASEAN's dominant and leading role and they are willing to accept ASEAN as the foundation of the future East Asia Economic Community through three ASEAN Plus One groupings (ASEAN plus China, ASEAN plus Japan and ASEAN plus South Korea), all with their respective FTAs. So, in the aspect of mechanism design, ASEAN becomes the axle country which gets more benefit, while the big countries become the spoke countries. ASEAN gets the dominant power as it seeks to protect and advance its interests.

Third, ASEAN is changing the traditional understanding about a country that seeks security. In the Cold War era, there were ceaseless wars in the Indochina peninsula which were not caused by ASEAN member countries. However, the old members of ASEAN, while there was no conflict between them, often had very strained relations. Since the Cold War, the steady expansion of ASEAN has finally extended peace to the whole of Southeast Asia. The ASEAN member states think that the traditional security threats come from the Korean Peninsula, the Taiwan Strait and the South China Sea. This ASEAN perception is the biggest motivating source pushing ASEAN's implementation of the strategy of balancing big powers. And this idea of ASEAN is also the main reason that ASEAN hopes that the Asia-Pacific big powers will, one by one, join the TAC, whose tenet is to resolve conflicts through peaceful means. In the past, larger powers always forced the small countries to sign peace treaties, while today larger powers join the TAC on their own initiative to give security assurances to the smaller nations.

Furthermore, ASEAN has demonstrated that it is receptive to the concept of 'human security' and of the need to think as a community of states in advancing this dimension of security. In the face of the transnational non-traditional security threats, these states are more fragile, their own national capacity is more obviously insufficient, and they urgently need regional and international cooperation. But they also worry more about the erosion of their national sovereignty. So the ASEAN states are making great efforts to seek the balancing-point among the national, regional and international community. ASEAN's preparedness to think more boldly about the absolutist conception of sovereignty and to take some initiatives that challenge it have also been a source of respect and, thus, power.

Fourth, ASEAN is changing the understanding of international norms. If we were to select the most engaging international norms in history, two strong candidates would be the 'peaceful co-existence' idea formulated during the Cold War era and the 'win–win' idea in the globalisation era. ASEAN members have realised peaceful co-existence among themselves, and now they are making a great effort to achieve 'win–win' outcomes with external powers. In their own region, ASEAN countries have found it impossible not to let the major powers win, which is the maximal reality in international politics and is also the original intention of its foreign strategy design. The tenet of ASEAN states is to realise a regional win: the small countries must seek independence, survival, development and might among big powers, which is the maximal reality of regional politics. From this point of view, ASEAN (whose *leitmotiv* is to seek to avoid conflicts and to seek common understanding) can gradually foster regional consciousness internally and also cautiously deal with the major powers externally. When ASEAN establishes the regional norms, it also creates the international norms, and the major powers are willing to abide by these international norms.

So, ASEAN is a power emerging in the region of East Asia.

Origins of ASEAN power

Where does ASEAN's new kind of power come from? And how has it been created? Its power mainly comes from the ASEAN organisation, its dominant role in the process of East Asia Cooperation, the balancing role it has played among big powers, and the norms it has helped to entrench.

The organisational power

The leaders of ASEAN states profoundly realise that only by pushing their integration rapidly and effectively can they strengthen their own competitive ability. For the 40-year history of ASEAN, its integration has generally been perceived by people as being rapid but not very effective. Four restricting factors are: (1) the new generation of leaders' relative lack of personal prestige and fascination compared to the old leaders such as Suharto, Lee Kuan Yew, and Mahathir. Most of the current leaders are locked into domestic affairs and relatively lack the enterprise and rallying point of pushing the integration; (2) ASEAN members have not yet formed a better coordinating mechanism—they still lack the common understanding and implementing ability in important strategic and security issues due, for example, to the Myanmar issue, increases in their own domestic divergences, and increases in the centrifugal trend; (3) ASEAN's economic integration might seem to have more benefits on paper, but this may not necessarily be more effective. Some ASEAN members are engaged in signing bilateral FTAs with outside regional powers, which may be causing Southeast Asia's economic integration process to slow; and (4) the society and civilians of every country lack a sufficient degree of identity towards ASEAN. The leaders of ASEAN member countries realise that the concept of ASEAN needs to be in the deep part of people's hearts, not simply just in the hearts of the bureaucracy and the elite classes. Civilians should be infused with a sense of belonging to ASEAN, so that a feeling of unification and related attitudes can take root.

So, at the end of 2003, at a milestone meeting, the leaders of ASEAN member states decided that they would build ASEAN as three communities: economic, security, and social and cultural. At the January 2007 ASEAN Cebu Summit, they decided to build the ASEAN Economic Community by 2015, ahead of schedule by five years and, at the same time, they passed the *ASEAN Charter Report* and started the constituting process of an *ASEAN Charter*. The above measures relate to the long-term blueprint, the institution-building, and cooperation in concrete fields respectively, in which there are four layers of deep meaning.

The first meaning is to ensure the development of Southeast Asia. If the ASEAN member states want to dominate this region, where major powers have struggled for dominance in the past, they have to realise 'united self-mightiness' based on national 'self-mightiness'. Every country keeps its own traditional characters at the same time it accelerates modernisation—this is 'self-mightiness'. Then every country makes use of ASEAN to develop collective power—this is 'united self-mightiness'. These two ways move forward together and support each other. This process was identified after the Second World War. Since the 1990s, ASEAN has begun to accelerate the integration process incessantly. At first it accelerated the process of ASEAN FTAs, and now it is beginning to accelerate the process of ASEAN community building.

The second meaning is to consolidate the power foundation of ASEAN. ASEAN has made great efforts to develop this foundation since the end of the Cold War in 1991. It has developed and implemented the strategy of balancing big powers and it has dominated the regional cooperation process in East Asia.

No single country of ASEAN could play such a role. It follows, of course, that the degree of ASEAN integration directly influences the sustainable development of its power.

The third meaning is to deal with the new challenges internally and externally. The 40-year process of ASEAN development has been a process of adjustment to deal with emerging challenges arising from internal and external transformations. Today, Asian structural changes caused by the rise of China and India, the non-traditional and transnational security problems such as terrorism, the Myanmar issue and other internal indigestion problems are evidence that ASEAN needs to further coordinate its internal relations and develop ways to resolve all these problems. Some out-moded principles and ways may be abandoned, while some new principles and ways that fit the new situations need affirmation and implementation. The advice given by the ASEAN Celebrity Group to the *ASEAN Charter* reflects this trend. The purpose of constituting the *ASEAN Charter* is to transform ASEAN from a loose organisation to one that is founded on certain legal mechanisms.

The fourth meaning is to strengthen the building of ASEAN's capacity to lead. In recent years, voices doubting and blaming ASEAN's leadership ability have been heard continually. If ASEAN wants to be a long-term leader, it needs to improve its ability to resolve its own problems (such as Myanmar); its coordinating ability to handle the relations of ASEAN, ASEAN Plus One, ASEAN Plus Three (APT), and ASEAN Plus Six groupings adeptly; and its ability to make long-term strategy, keep strategic initiative and creativity, continue to play a greater role among major powers, and avoid being marginalised.

From this point of view, it would be better to say that ASEAN is enduring the feeling of crisis caused by power, rather than to say it is enjoying the glory of power. This is the original driving force of the ASEAN integration process. This process shoulders so many missions that it directly relates to the destiny and future of East Asia cooperation. So it remains the right choice for China, Japan, South Korea and other East Asia big powers to continue to support the building of ASEAN integration, and to continue to support ASEAN as the driver of East Asia cooperation.

The dominant power

The question of who will be the dominant power in the process of East Asia cooperation is the perennial focus of debate. A dominant power means some country or organisation which plays the dominant role and has the ability to design the direction, manage the process, and coordinate the relations for East Asian cooperation. According to this standard, the dominant power of East Asian cooperation could take four possible forms.

The first possibility is that China and Japan will dominate together. According to the experience whereby France and Germany played the dominant role in the European Union, some scholars suppose that, in the future, only China and Japan will have the ability to dominate the process of East Asia cooperation. If these two countries could go forward hand-in-hand, it would be East Asia's good fortune. But, since 1997, this possibility has not appeared; and as long as China-Japan relations cannot be improved, the chance of the two giants proceeding hand-in-hand is slim.

The second possibility is that China and Japan will struggle to be the dominant power. The developing trends of the two countries are very clear: China is rising to become a strong comprehensive power in East Asia, while Japan is developing to become a normal power in East Asia. Some experts think that the two regional powers both want to be the 'big brother' in East Asia and that the future will be characterised by structural confrontation and competition between the two sides. In regional cooperation, their competing relations are to struggle for the dominant power of East Asia cooperation. Such a possibility can do nothing but exacerbate the China-Japan conflicts and the strained atmosphere in East Asia, which could cause unease among Southeast Asian countries. Nor is it likely to attract US support, even if America's bigger worry is that its own hegemony in East Asia will be supplanted by Japan and China together.

The third possibility is that China and Japan will infiltrate the region to dominate it. Some scholars think that, on the issue of the dominant power concerning East Asia, China and Japan may change open strife to in-fighting. In this scenario, the two sides would seek to influence the East Asia cooperation process respectively through the Southeast Asian countries by having close relations with these countries separately. But this mode is complex and ineffective because of ASEAN's consensus principle.

The fourth possibility is that all East Asian countries publicly (together) push ASEAN to be the dominant power. If either China or Japan sought this role, it would encounter resistance from the other. So, ASEAN could be anointed as the best available entity acceptable to China, Japan and the United States, to drive East Asia cooperation.

ASEAN is always playing the roles of designer, pusher and organiser in the process of East Asian cooperation. It implements the strategy of balancing big powers and tries hard to be impartial among big powers. According to George Yeo, Singapore's Foreign Minister, 'we are not the potential competitor of big powers either'. The strength of ASEAN is inferior to the strength of China or Japan, so it is difficult to reach common understanding and become the regional leader. But ASEAN insists on pushing the cadence of East Asian cooperation according to the comfortable degree principle, and this is a fit for the diversity of East Asia. Even the United States, which wanders outside the East Asia cooperation, also (according to former US Secretary of State Condoleezza Rice) thinks that ASEAN should be the leader of the East Asia Cooperation. Finally, India, Australia and New Zealand (all new members of the EAS) need ASEAN to coordinate relations.

The balancing power

After the end of the Cold War, ASEAN became aware that the one-power-dominant structure would not lead to regional stability and prosperity. Instead, in order to maintain these, ASEAN needed to develop a strategy to draw all the major powers into the region while it manoeuvred among them. The big powers would strengthen their strategic presence in the region, while simultaneously acting as a check and balance on each other. Obviously, ASEAN would be the biggest winner under this structure. For a long time, ASEAN has developed its bilateral relations with the major powers under the mechanism of Comprehensive Dialogue Partnerships, leading to the formation of several ASEAN Plus One groupings. So far, ASEAN has laid the strategic structure of balancing big powers by and large, with itself as the 'core'. ASEAN has built ASEAN Plus One cooperative mechanisms with China, Japan, South Korea, India, Australia, New Zealand, the European Union, Russia, and the United States. Also, ASEAN has negotiated or is negotiating with these powers the establishment of FTAs. Moreover, ASEAN has persuaded all Asia-Pacific powers except the United States to sign the TAC. So, we can conclude that ASEAN has created a relationship structure in the Asia-Pacific region that resembles a Chinese folding-fan, with ASEAN as the joint point of the ribs of the fan, while those ASEAN Plus One mechanisms are the supportive ribs. That is the basic structure under which ASEAN can carry out its strategy of balancing big powers.

The functional logic of ASEAN's strategy of balancing big powers is as follows. While ASEAN is building the strategic folding-fan, it is also providing channels for regional powers to realise their interests in the Southeast Asia region. In the past, big powers scrambled for spheres of influence in the region and tended to contest with hard or realist means. Now, ASEAN members hope to maintain equal, peaceful and co-existent relations with big powers in the region. As a result, through a series of new regional mechanisms, ASEAN leaders are trying to admit big powers into the Southeast Asian region in a peaceful, friendly and 'win–win' way, endowing the idealistic folding-fan with realistic effects. The main mechanistic measures are that: (1) ASEAN develops partnerships with big powers so as to strengthen political mutual trust and friendship; (2) big powers sign the TAC at ASEAN's urging, thereby making them legally committed to not using armed force in the region; and (3) ASEAN builds FTAs with big powers respectively, leading to profound interdependent relationships. Due to the fact that ASEAN is the initiator and participant of all those various mechanisms, it will be more informed than other powers and it will develop the mechanisms with different powers as need and opportunity arise. So, ASEAN can fully make use of the two advantages to carry out strategies for its own benefit. For example, it is carrying out FTA negotiations with China, India, South Korea, Australia and New Zealand respectively. Because there is no coordination among these powers and they are negotiating different timetables with ASEAN, ASEAN can take advantage of all relevant information in the negotiations and make optimal evaluations, either to raise its negotiating price or to raise its status in international relations.

The normative power

At first, some former leaders of Asian countries (such as Singapore's Lee Kuan Yew and Malaysia's Mahathir) advocated the concept of 'Asian Values'. Then there emerged the 'ASEAN Way', which promoted the development of regional cooperation in East Asia. In any event, all these affect the regional trend of thought. In particular, the 'ASEAN Way' and East Asian Regionalism appear more consistent with the complexity and diversity in East Asia and more acceptable to international society. The 'ASEAN Way' emphasises the principles of negotiation, consensus and comfort, while East Asian Regionalism is open.

In her famous book titled *The Retreat of the State: The Diffusion of Power in the World Economy*, Susan Strange argued that, in the era of economic globalisation, power derives from the interaction of the following four structures: security, production, finance and knowledge. Strange's theory of structural interaction reinforces the argument advanced above on how ASEAN countries may obtain power.[3] ASEAN members shape a new regional security structure through regional cooperation and a strategy of balancing powers; they build a new regional production structure based on ASEAN's role as 'wheel and axle'; they create a regional finance structure to protect the financial security of small countries through East Asia cooperation; and they establish a new regional norm structure through perfecting and practising the 'ASEAN Way'. In essence, structure leads to power, though the solidity (consistence) of this kind of power remains an open question.

ASEAN has obtained the following four strategic benefits: (1) the impression of a poor and backward Southeast Asia which was the target of sphere of influence competition among the big powers has been replaced by a new ASEAN that impresses with its equal and peaceful coexistence with the big countries in the region; (2) economic interdependence has been deepened and regional economic cooperation has been guided by building FTAs with the big powers; (3) a commitment by the big powers on the solution of conflicts without resorting to armed force has been introduced, by the signing of the TAC by all major Asia-Pacific countries except the United States (France (from the European Union) joined the TAC in January 2007); and (4) manoeuvring, checking and balancing among the big countries stimulates them to attach greater importance to Southeast Asian states and, hence, to increase their respective strategic inputs.

All of these benefits for ASEAN are, in turn, conducive to the stability and prosperity of the region and to establishing the new model of international relationships.

ASEAN power and China

For the ASEAN countries, being surrounded by the big powers is an unalterable geographical reality. At the same time, ASEAN can change or shape its strategic environment. ASEAN can co-dance harmoniously with the big powers by relying on the concerted efforts from within together with the international situation, as well as via creating and implementing both the strategy of 'check and balance' among those powers and the strategy of East Asia cooperation. As a result, a regional new order can be established that features peace and prosperity. Along this course, China can offer help and support to ASEAN to fulfil its goals and resolve its problems, so as to achieve a 'win–win' outcome in the region.

Put another way, the success of ASEAN in forging a new security framework to a large extent relies on strategic support from China, which is a firm supporter of ASEAN integration. While some countries seek to dominate the process of East Asian cooperation, China is actively maintaining the leadership status of ASEAN. China was the first big power to negotiate the establishment of FTAs with ASEAN, to join TAC, to establish a strategic partnership with ASEAN, and to bring 'smile diplomacy' to Southeast Asia. It also hopes to become the first to sign the *Treaty on the Southeast Asia Nuclear Weapon Free Zone*. The positive role of China has drawn other counterparts to show their goodwill to ASEAN, which has enabled the proper performance of the balance strategy and the regional cooperation strategy of ASEAN. With the joint efforts of China and ASEAN, other powers have begun to approach Southeast Asia in a similar manner, so as to achieve cooperation, a 'win–win' outcome, and equality, which is objectively conducive to multipolarity in the region. To help others and to achieve this 'win–win' outcome at the same time, the China-ASEAN relationship has become a good example of how to develop and handle international relationships.

Over the past 15 years, having helped ASEAN tide over the 1997–98 Asian financial crisis and the Severe Acute Respiratory Syndrome (SARS) outbreak, China then attempted to control the H5N1 influenza through joint efforts with ASEAN. Over the next 15 years, the risks confronting ASEAN from modernisation and globalisation will not diminish. For China, the next 15 years will also be a period in which strategic opportunities and protruding contradictions abound. The deepening strategic partnership between China and ASEAN calls for sharing the risks as well as the gains. In the future, the joint mission for the two sides will be how to avoid strategic risks and take economic and social risks under control. In essence, as China helps extricate ASEAN from risks and worries, a 'win–win' outcome for the region can also be achieved.

Judged from the development of bilateral relations between ASEAN and China since the end of the Cold War, China and ASEAN have achieved a 'win–win' relationship. China's relations with ASEAN and with ASEAN's members respectively have all reached the most positive point in history. The two sides witnessed positive developments simultaneously in many aspects: the coincidence of China's rise and ASEAN's ascendant status in the international community; and the coincidence of China's greater influence and ASEAN's more dominant role in the region. In a word, ASEAN and China go forward in tandem. The phrase 'Strategic Partnership Relationship' indicates that China's relations with ASEAN as a whole have risen to an unprecedented height, which will not be surpassed by China's relations with other regions.

The progress of China-ASEAN relations brings the feelings of stability, sureness and accomplishment to China's neighbour policy. This is the first time that such feelings have characterised China's relations with Southeast Asia. The benefits from this good relationship are wide-ranging: China can deal with the North Korean problem, China-Japan relations and the Taiwan issue attentively; it can, together with ASEAN, promote the development of East Asia regional cooperation, or even pan-Asian cooperation including Central Asia and South Asia; and it can associate itself with ASEAN's strategy of balancing powers in a natural way, and thus reduce the worrisome attitudes of other powers (such as the United States and Japan) toward China. Meanwhile, ASEAN has gained weight and influence from its good relationship with China. For example, China supports the process of integration within ASEAN and its dominant role in the development of East Asian cooperation on the basis that this does not harm the interests of other regions. This kind of relationship is a comparatively stable situation, resulting from complex interactions in a global context. As a result, there is great rationality and vitality within this relationship.

In view of the above, China's future strategy should include the following points. First, China should continue to support ASEAN's process of integration, and seek to link it with the three communities within ASEAN, which are still in the construction phase. Second, China should advocate ASEAN's dominant role in the development of the East Asia Cooperation, and realise China's own strategic interests while helping ASEAN to achieve the ideal regional structure. Third, China should be fully aware that it is only one part of ASEAN's strategy of balancing major powers. In future, big powers, such as the United States, Japan, India and Australia will definitely increase their strategic presence in this region. In this circumstance, China should not treat other regional powers as enemies or exclude other big power interests from the region. Rather, China should share its interests with the other big powers in the region.

ENDNOTES

[1] Pang Zhongying article available at <http://news.sina.com.cn/w/2005-12-12/10248559207.shtml>, accessed 5 May 2008.

[2] This chapter was written before mid-2009. On 22 July 2009, US Secretary of State Hillary Clinton signed the United States' 'Instrument of Accession to the Treaty of Amity and Cooperation in Southeast Asia'. The 10 ASEAN Foreign Ministers then signed an 'Instrument of Extension of the Treaty of Amity and Cooperation in Southeast Asia', completing US accession to TAC.

[3] See Susan Strange, *The Retreat of the State: The Diffusion of Power in the World Economy*, Cambridge University Press, Cambridge, 2000.

Chapter 4

The SCO's Success in Security Architecture

Pan Guang

The Shanghai Cooperation Organisation (SCO) is now showing a more active posture in safeguarding security and promoting economic-cultural development in the region, being cognisant of the situation in areas around Central Asia like East Asia, the Middle East and South Asia, and demonstrating that the SCO, barely eight years old, has embarked on a new course of pragmatic development.

Achievements in maintaining security in the heart of Eurasia

Since 1996, the process of the 'Shanghai Five—SCO' has registered some remarkable achievements in security cooperation. Its major accomplishments include three outcomes.

First, confidence-building measures have been put in place, leading finally to the resolution of the border problems left over from history. Within the frameworks of the 'Shanghai Five'—SCO, and due to the joint efforts of China, Russia, Kazakhstan, Kyrgyzstan and Tajikistan, all the disputes regarding the Western section of the former China-Soviet border of more than 3000 km—a border that had bred instability and conflict for centuries—were completely solved in six years. This was a rare accomplishment in the history of international relations.

Second, there has been close cooperation in the struggle against destabilising trans-border elements. After the breakup of the Soviet Union and the emergence of the Taliban in Afghanistan, extremist and terrorist forces started acting rampantly in the Central Asia, causing big trouble for countries in this region. The 'Shanghai Five' was the first international organisation to call for cooperative action against terrorism in Central Asia. On 15 June 2001, less than three months before the 11 September 2001 terrorist attacks on the United States, leaders of the six founding states of the SCO signed the *Shanghai Convention on Combating Terrorism, Separatism and Extremism*. This Convention, as the first international treaty on anti-terrorism in the twenty-first century, spelt out the legal framework for SCO members to fight terrorism and other evil forces, and for their coordination with other countries. Within the framework of the Convention,

SCO member states cooperated and established the Regional Anti-Terrorist Structure (RATS) to combat and contain extremism and terrorism in the region.

Third, the SCO has been able to restrain conflicts from spreading and to maintain regional security and stability. The ethnic and religious conflicts and issues that history left to Central Asia are as intricate and complex as those in the Balkans and the Middle East. Fortunately, the establishment of the SCO mechanism proved to be the defining difference for Central Asia, providing this region with a more positive outlook than either the Balkans or the Middle East. Within its framework, Central Asia managed to restrain malignant conflicts like the civil war in Afghanistan from spreading in the region as has happened in the Balkans and the Middle East. The SCO established a successful model for the troubled international scene after the end of the Cold War. One can say without exaggeration that, in the absence of the 'Shanghai Five–SCO', the Taliban may have continued marching northwards, and the conflict in Afghanistan could have possibly spread to neighbouring countries as well. In this regard, one can say that the SCO is playing an essential role in maintaining regional security and stability.

Taking a wider view, all these abovementioned successes, achieved within the 'Shanghai Five–SCO' framework, have been of strategic significance not only for the member states and for the security and development of Central Asia overall, but also for the peace and development in areas around Central Asia such as East Asia, the Middle East and South Asia and, indeed, even globally.

Economic and cultural development: a solid basis for security cooperation

The SCO leadership has placed emphasis on promoting economic and cultural cooperation, believing that such cooperation constitutes not only the basis of political and security cooperation, but serves directly the long-term development and broader interests of future generations in the region. The SCO summit meeting in Tashkent, Uzbekistan, pointed out that

> maintaining a sustained economic growth in Central Asia and the countries in its periphery and meeting the urgent needs of their peoples serves as a major guarantee for ensuring the stability and security of the region and the countries in its periphery.[1]

The SCO summit meeting in Astana, Kazakhstan, made it clear that the main priority for the near future was to put into practice the Action Plan on Fulfillment of the Program of Multilateral Trade and Economic Cooperation between SCO member states, thus embarking on a pragmatic course of cooperation in, for example, trade, transportation, environmental protection, disaster relief, and the rational use of natural resources. At the 2006 SCO summit meeting in Shanghai, China, members decided to choose energy, information technology, and transportation as the priority areas for economic cooperation,[2] stressing particularly the importance for proceeding with the implementation of certain demonstration programs in these areas. The SCO Mechanism of Inter-bank Cooperation—the first step to the SCO Development Bank to be formally inaugurated before the Shanghai summit—was expected to provide a financing platform for major projects in the region. The official launch of the SCO Business Council during the Shanghai summit will provide a new source for facilitating greater economic cooperation within the SCO framework.[3]

In respect of cultural cooperation, SCO member states have actively cooperated in the SCO framework on education, culture, sports, tourism, and other cultural endeavours. Chinese President Hu Jintao has always stressed the need for humanistic cooperation. As he pointed out at the SCO Tashkent summit:

> SCO members all have their distinctive humanistic resources that make up good potentials for cooperation. Cooperation should be actively promoted in fields of culture, education, science and technology, tourism, mass media, etc. so as to enhance the mutual understanding and friendship among the SCO peoples, and consolidate the social basis of growth of SCO.[4]

Especially noteworthy is the point mentioned at the Astana summit: 'Formulation of coordinated methods and recommendations on conducting prophylactic activities and respective explanatory work among the public in order to confront attempts at exerting a destructive influence on public opinion is a vital task.'[5] The Shanghai summit emphasised again the need to promote substantially both people-to-people and cultural cooperation. In the short run, the focus of such cooperation is to highlight the spirit of the Silk Road by enhancing the mutual communication and understanding among different civilisations and nations in the region, so as to strengthen the emotional ties among the Chinese, Central Asians and Russians, and also to pave the way for the unfolding comprehensive cooperation within the SCO. The document on educational cooperation signed at the Shanghai summit is another SCO initiative to broaden both its people-to-people and cultural cooperation, while the formal launch of the SCO Forum—an academic mechanism of research and discussion before the Shanghai summit—will provide intellectual support to the further development of the organisation.[6] The first and second SCO Cultural and Art Festival held during the Astana and Shanghai summits have also shown themselves as specific achievements in this field.

Response to new challenges

Since the beginning of 2005, there has been a wave of 'election-related turmoil' or so-called 'Colour Revolution' in Central Asia, with terrorist and extremist forces fishing in troubled waters. In Afghanistan, a new wave of Iraq-style terrorist attacks has signalled the resurgence of the Taliban and al-Qaeda. More ominously, Hizb-ut-Tahrir (the Islamic Party of Liberation) and other extreme groups are fast gaining support in Central Asia, particularly in the poverty-stricken Fergana countryside, bespeaking a re-emerging grim security situation in the region that poses new challenges for the SCO.

Facing such a serious situation, the SCO Astana summit in 2005 took the initiative in shouldering chief responsibility for safeguarding security in Central Asia. The heads of the states decided to increase significantly the security cooperation on the basis of the achievements made so far, including particularly the following measures:

a. promoting close cooperation among the diplomatic, foreign economic, law-enforcing, national defence and special-mission authorities of the member states;
b. working out effective measures and institutions to respond collectively to those developments that threaten regional peace, security and stability;
c. coordinating the security-ensuring laws and regulations in the member states;
d. cooperating in researching and developing new technologies and equipment for coping with new challenges and threats;
e. establishing new effective structures in the mass media arena to deal with new challenges and threats;
f. combating the smuggling of weapons, ammunitions, explosives as well as drugs, and fighting organised transnational crime, illegal immigration and mercenary troops activities;
g. giving special attention to the prevention of terrorists using weapons of mass destruction and their launching vehicles;
h. taking precautionary measures against cyber-terrorism; and
i. drafting uniform approaches and standards for monitoring financial flows to individuals and organisations suspected of terrorist sympathies.

It was also believed that cooperation on drug trafficking should become a focus as defined by the previous SCO agreement on fighting the illegal trafficking in narcotics and their precursors. It was resolved that the SCO should specifically step up its participation in the international efforts on the formation of an 'anti-drug belt' around Afghanistan, and in formulating special programs to assist Afghan authorities to stabilise the country's social, economic and humanitarian situation.

Especially conspicuous has been the following words quoted from the Declaration of the SCO Astana summit:

> Today we are noticing the positive dynamics of stabilizing the internal political situation in Afghanistan. A number of the SCO member states provided their ground infrastructure for temporary stationing of military

contingents of some states, members of the coalition, as well as their territory and air space for military transit in the interest of anti-terrorist cooperation. Considering the completion of the active military stage of anti-terrorist operation in Afghanistan, the member states of the Shanghai Cooperation Organization consider it necessary that respective members of the antiterrorist coalition set a final timeline for their temporary use of the above-mentioned objects of infrastructure and stay of their military contingents on the territories of the SCO member states.[7]

Three points should be emphasised. First, these remarks are not specifically targeted at the United States, but more broadly at 'respective members of the anti-terrorist coalition'; in other words, at all those countries and international organisations that use the infrastructure facilities of SCO countries or station their troops in SCO countries. Second, the SCO has voiced its views and suggestions, while any final arrangements still have to be worked out through multilateral or bilateral consultations between SCO states and those relevant parties. Third, as the situation in Afghanistan remains severe, this is not the right time to formulate a timetable for the withdrawal of all foreign troops from Central Asia. Indeed, it is necessary to step up anti-terror activities in Central Asia and strengthen the anti-terror ties among the SCO, the United States, the European Union and other parties.

It was decided at the 2006 SCO Shanghai summit to deepen cooperation in security affairs. It stressed: 'To comprehensively deepen cooperation in combating terrorism, separatism, extremism and drug trafficking is a priority area for SCO.'[8] It was therefore deemed imperative to continue the construction of RATS, to launch anti-terror joint exercises, and to establish an anti-drugs mechanism. This summit pointed out for the first time that SCO members prohibit any individual or group from conducting on their territories any kind of activity that would undermine the interests of other members. Following the proposition made at the Astana summit to 'establish effective mechanisms in the mass media for coping with new challenges and new threats', the summit witnessed the signing of 'the Statement of Heads of Member States of the Shanghai Cooperation Organisation On International Information Security' and the decision to establish a commission of information security experts to lay the groundwork for the drafting and implementation of related action plans. In Shanghai, the leaders also instructed the Council of National Coordinators to conduct consultations on concluding a multilateral legal document on long-term neighbourly and amicable cooperation within the SCO framework.[9]

Strategic significance of the SCO for the security architecture of Asia

The SCO, as an open organisation, is achieving the development of fruitful multilateral cooperation with all the states and international organisations on the basis of the principles of equality and mutual benefit. The 'Regulation on the Status of Observer to the Shanghai Cooperation Organisation', accepted during the June 2004 Tashkent summit, is the first document concerning contacts between the SCO and the outside world, which has important significance for the promotion of international cooperation, as well as the development of the Organisation itself. In December 2004 the SCO was granted observer status in the General Assembly of the United Nations. In April 2005 the SCO signed the Memorandum of Understanding with ASEAN and the Commonwealth of Independent States, establishing a relationship of cooperation and partnership. In September 2005 SCO Secretary-General Zhang Deguang was invited to address the UN Summit, dedicated to the sixtieth anniversary of its establishment. This was an important sign of the maturity and international prestige of the SCO. It is important to note that the SCO granted observer status to Mongolia, Pakistan, Iran and India, which increased the potential opportunities of cooperation and broadened the prospects for SCO development.

The strategic significance of the SCO's success for the security architecture in Asia has a number of dimensions.

First, the SCO has contributed to confidence-building and stability in Asia. It has increased confidence-building and mutual trust among its members and observers—especially between China and her nine close neighbours, including Uzbekistan and Iran with whom China shares no borders. The borders that China shares with seven SCO members and observers takes up about three quarters of China's total land border—14 799 km. When peace and security is maintained in such massive border areas, the peoples in the region no longer feel exposed to direct military threats. Meanwhile, when it boasts over half of the world's population with such large members and observers like Russia, China and India, the SCO exerts a much larger influence over a major part of the Eurasian landmass.

Second, the SCO has provided a very positive example to the rest of Asia in solving complicated issues left over by history. By resolving in a matter of several years the century-old border problems between China and the states of the former Soviet Union, the approach adopted by the SCO (of mutual trust, disarmament and cooperative security) may provide a model that can be adapted to other outstanding border problems such as those between China and India, between India and Pakistan, among Central Asian states, and with respect to the South China Sea dispute and the China-Japan dispute over the Diaoyutai Islands and part of the East China Sea.

Third, the SCO's anti-terror campaign is strategically important for anti-terror cooperation in Asia. In the new surge of terrorist attacks sweeping the world following the 2003 Iraq War, the formation of an 'arc of terrorism'—a 'belt' stretching from the Middle East, Central Asia and South Asia to Southeast Asia—is a most disturbing development. What is particularly worrying is that Southeast Asia, sitting at the eastern end of this 'belt', has become a high-risk area of frequent terrorist attacks in recent years. Lee Kuan Yew, Minister Mentor in the Singapore Cabinet, has remarked that it is very disturbing to see that, although the 230 million Muslims in Southeast Asia have long been 'tolerant and easy to live with', recent changes indicate that extremism and terrorism are seeking their opportunities among them. Certain terrorist groups closely connected to al-Qaeda (like Jemaah Islamiyah, Kumpulan Mujahidin Malaysia, and Abu Sayyaf) have plotted a series of terrorist activities. If the maritime terrorist activities in Southeast Asia affect the security of the Strait of Malacca, which is indeed a very realistic possibility, East Asia's energy security will be threatened, as 60–70 percent of East Asia's imported oil goes through the Strait. It is clear that the terrorist groups in Southeast Asia are closely connected with terrorist organisations in Central Asia and South Asia, particularly so in terms of intellectual connections, organisational networks, and approaches to activities, and by all functioning within one international terrorist network. For this reason, the SCO's success and its protracted efforts in combating terrorism are strategically important for the anti-terror campaign in Asia as a whole.

Fourth, the SCO's energy cooperation has strategic significance for energy security in Asia. After several years of construction, the oil pipeline from Kazakhstan to China became operational in 2006. This new pipeline will develop into the SCO's multilateral energy cooperation project involving Russia and other Central Asian countries. The designed handling capacity of the pipeline is 20 million tonnes per year, which will be a big jump over the annual amount of 500 thousand tonnes currently handled on railways. Gas pipelines from Central Asia and Siberia to China will also be constructed. If connected with the Xinjiang–Shanghai Gas Pipeline, the Central Asia–China lines will also help the implementation of the Energy Eastward Transportation Program. Japan and South Korea, which can also take part in this project, will be entitled to part of the gas transported by the lines. This will open a new chapter in energy cooperation between East Asia and Central Asia. It should be pointed out that Central Asia and Siberia, as distinct from the Middle East, Africa and Latin America, are sources of energy supply that demand no protection from any blue-water navy. As East Asian countries are still unable, for the foreseeable future, to develop the naval power necessary to protect long oil shipping lines, this sole alternative to maritime transportation is of crucial strategic significance for East Asia's energy security and overall development. Likewise, for the first time in history, Central Asian countries obtained an eastward energy pipeline, which is not going through Russia, or the Caucasus or the Middle East, but crossing China, and finally reaching the Pacific Ocean. Obviously, this pipeline is strategically important for the future development of Asia.

In any case, making the fight against drug trafficking and cross-border crimes its top priority, signing a joint declaration on maintaining the international information security, giving full attention to environmental protection and the protective development of water resources, and other endeavours, all highlight the broad perspective that the SCO adopts when viewing and implementing security cooperation. Keeping an open mind on the various non-conventional security issues as well as the conventional ones in the framework of the SCO makes not only Central Asia and South Asia but also East Asia and Southeast Asia better positioned to play a growing role in global comprehensive security cooperation.

Looking ahead: big tasks and a long journey

In June 2006, the heads of the SCO member states and observer states gathered in Shanghai to celebrate and review the 5-year process following the establishment of the Shanghai Cooperation Organisation and the 10-year process following the initiation of the 'Shanghai Five'. The leaders discussed the new developments in the international arena and in Central Asia, and its impact on the SCO. As mentioned above, they have put forward the strategic goal to construct a 'harmonious Central Asia' and proposed an ambitious plan for the next stage of SCO development.

In looking to the future, it is necessary to highlight the fact that the SCO still faces several major issues which merit urgent attention.

It is essential to accelerate the process of economic cooperation within the SCO. Three factors are extremely important to realise this aim. The first is to be pragmatic in designing cooperation goals and in implementing the cooperation measures. Empty talk and a lack of specific goals and effective measures will never result in success, particularly when it comes to economic issues. The second point is to persist in following such market rules as a level playing field, equality and reciprocity, mutual opening, and a combination of both bilateral and multilateral approaches. Caring only about one's own interests is a mistake, while detaching cooperation from the market base is even more so. Additionally, bilateral cooperation and multilateral cooperation can be mutually enhancing—the oil pipeline between Kazakhstan and China, for example, is now giving rise to a triangular energy cooperation involving Russia as well. The third point is to move ahead with coordination and priorities for each stage. Up-front investment is certainly necessary, yet participants must guard against excessive expansion and repetitive construction.

There is an obvious need to deepen security cooperation. A joint advantage of the SCO in the near future will still be in the security area. Yet, there must be a deepening of the cooperation in this aspect if the organisation is to make headway on the basis of past achievements. Several practical steps suggest themselves: (1) RATS should be quickly consolidated to work efficiently, and specific cooperation should be stepped up in drafting an SCO list of wanted terrorists and terrorist groups, and in regularising joint anti-terror exercises; (2) a proposed Central Asian Nuclear-Free Zone (CANFZ) program should be taken forward, so that the region can avoid the proliferation of weapons of mass destruction and the associated risk of an arms race; and (3) further campaigns should be launched to crack down on drug trafficking and, as mentioned before, achieve active participation in the UN action to establish an anti-drug 'belt' around Afghanistan for the peaceful reconstruction of the country. Only once practical steps are taken to consolidate established initiatives can the SCO play an indispensable role in maintaining security in the whole Central Asian region as well as in its member states.

It should be pointed out that there is great potential for anti-terror cooperation between the SCO and other Asian countries and organisations. They can be specifically described as follows: a joint research program on anti-terror; a joint training program on anti-terror; joint anti-terror exercises (search, rescue, quick response); the promotion of reconstruction in post-war Afghanistan; an exchange of information on terrorism in East Asia, South Asia, Southeast Asia and Central Asia; and counter transnational criminal programs focusing on thwarting activities such as weapons smuggling, drug trafficking and illegal immigration.

Cultural cooperation should be pushed forward steadily. The existing bilateral cultural cooperation among the SCO member states should be expanded into multilateral cultural cooperation within the SCO framework, which certainly calls for organisational coordination, financial support, and professional programming. In the near future, the cooperation will specifically unfold on many fronts, including exchanging mutual visits by cultural, artistic and sporting groups; hosting joint art festivals and exhibitions; dispatching and accepting more exchange students; promoting visits by high-level experts and scholars; mutually assisting in training talents in various fields; increasing cultural exchanges among young people; and facilitating culture-oriented tourism along the Silk Road.

External exchange and augmentation of the organisation should be handled judiciously. After Mongolia, Pakistan, Iran and India were accepted as SCO observers, more and more countries have expressed their wish to become SCO observers, join the SCO or cooperate with the SCO. In light of these growing requests, the Shanghai summit has commissioned the SCO Secretariat to monitor the implementation of the documents on cooperation between the SCO and other organisations, and to facilitate the actual work of cooperation between the SCO and its observer states. The heads of state have also entrusted the SCO Council of Member State Coordinators to make suggestions regarding the procedures for accepting new members.[10] It remains a major challenge for the SCO to sort out its relationship with such important players as the United States, the European Union, and Japan which, although unlikely to be interested in becoming members or observers of the SCO, nonetheless offer great potential as partners. One way is to establish, aside from the formal members and observers, the category of partner states, modelled after the North Atlantic Treaty Organization (NATO)'s Partnership for Peace. One country, for example, might become an SCO partner for anti-terror or an SCO partner for anti-drug cooperation. Indeed, Afghanistan has already become a fully active partner of the SCO. Whether immediately feasible or not, these moves are worthy of careful consideration when broadening the external exchange and attempting cautious enlargement of the SCO.

Conclusion

In reviewing the successful journey that the SCO has undertaken and examining its future development, the following points merit special attention. First, regional cooperation must be steadily institutionalised, and be guaranteed by relevant international or regional laws and regulations. At the same time, the discrepancy in rules and regulations between the domestic and the regional should be sorted out in a careful manner. Second, regional security cooperation must be based on 'comprehensive security', and, particularly, the handling of conventional security threats should be combined closely with the handling of non-conventional security threats. And finally, it must be remembered that the maintenance of regional security and stability and regional economic and cultural cooperation are closely interdependent. Each facilitates the other.

ENDNOTES

[1] The Tashkent Declaration from the Shanghai Cooperation Organisation summit in Tashkent, Uzbekistan, 17 June 2004.

[2] *Joint Communiqué of the Meeting of the Council of Heads of Member States of the Shanghai Cooperation Organisation*, Shanghai, 15 June 2006, available at <http://china.org.cn/english/features/meeting/171590.htm>, accessed 17 June 2009. The 2007 meeting of the Council of Member States of the Shanghai Cooperation Organisation took place on 16 August 2007 at Bishkek, Kyrgyzstan. The Joint Communiqué is available at <http://www.sectsco.org/news_detail.asp?id=1721&LanguageID=2>, accessed 5 May 2008.

[3] *Joint Communiqué of the Meeting of the Council of Heads of Member States of the Shanghai Cooperation Organisation*, Shanghai, 15 June 2006.

[4] President Hu Jintao's speech at the Tashkent Summit, Uzbekistan, 17 June 2004.

[5] *Declaration of Heads of Member States of Shanghai Cooperation Organisation*, Astana, Kazakhstan, 6 July 2005.

[6] The SCO Secretariat, *The SCO Bulletin*, Beijing, 2006, p. 57.

[7] *Declaration of Heads of Member States of Shanghai Cooperation Organisation*, Astana, 6 July 2005.

[8] *Declaration on the Fifth Anniversary of the Shanghai Cooperation Organisation*, Shanghai, 15 June 2006, available at <http://english.scosummit2006.org/en_zxbb/2006-06/15/content_755.htm>, accessed 17 June 2009.

[9] *Joint Communiqué of the Meeting of the Council of Heads of Member States of the Shanghai Cooperation Organisation*, Shanghai, 15 June 2006.

[10] *Joint Communiqué of the Meeting of the Council of Heads of Member States of the Shanghai Cooperation Organisation*, Shanghai, 15 June 2006.

Chapter 5

Shifting Tides: China and North Korea

Zhu Feng

The decision by Kim Jong-il's regime to test-launch missiles in July 2006 and to test a nuclear device on 9 October 2006, dramatically impacted China's foreign policy toward North Korea.[1] These incidents served to undermine the Six-Party Talks hosted by China, and threatened to further exacerbate the forces destabilising regional security in Northeast Asia. Pyongyang's defiance of China's stern warnings regarding these tests finally signalled to Beijing that the 'North Korea crisis' was deteriorating catastrophically.

Following both the missile and nuclear tests, China voted in favour of United Nations Security Council (UNSC) Resolutions 1695, 1705 and 1718, clearly indicating that Beijing was seeking new policies to deal with North Korea. Today, there remains a degree of internal discussion on what that policy direction should be and the nature of China's relations with North Korea. For a variety of reasons, a residual sympathy for North Korea remains in China which is preventing a showdown between Beijing and Pyongyang. Yet China is decisively working to expand its cooperation with the international community to force North Korea to discontinue its pursuit of nuclear weapons and lower the threat arising from its Weapons of Mass Destruction (WMD). Furthermore, if China's own complex domestic and international cost-benefit calculus can be untangled, a significant shift in Beijing's policy—entailing abandonment of its patron relationship with North Korea and coercion to roll back North Korea's nuclear capabilities—may be just around the corner.

Missile tests: A turning point

North Korea's last three missile tests conducted since the outbreak of the North Korean nuclear crisis in October 2002 had limited diplomatic impact, mainly because the test launches involved only short-range or shore-based anti-ship missiles.[2] Since North Korea already possessed such missile capabilities, there was no evidence that North Korean missile technology had improved substantively since the *Taepodong-1* was test-fired in 1998. However, when intelligence confirmed that North Korea was going to test-fire long-range missiles in June 2006—missiles capable of reaching the west coast of the United States—reactions by the United States and Japan fundamentally changed. These tests were also significant because they damaged China's credibility as an impartial mediator and decreased its presumed influence on North Korea.

Following the long-range missile tests on 5 July 2006, an intense debate arose in the United States regarding the possibility of using a preemptive strike capability on North Korean missile facilities. Although such a strike was ultimately ruled out by the White House, the United States announced that the missile defence system in Alaska would enter a higher alert level. In addition, the United States and Japan decided to deploy missile defences in Japan, and the United States sent its only *Aegis* cruiser equipped with a marine missile defence system into the offshore waters of North Korea. All these moves point to a marked escalation of the military confrontation revolving around the North Korean missile launch—a situation China had been working to avoid with its mediation efforts in the North Korean nuclear crisis and by hosting the Six-Party Talks.

The possibility of North Korea's long-range missile tests did not at first draw a particularly swift or strong response from China, as it has grown accustomed to such threatening tactics from North Korea whenever the Six-Party Talks stagnate and China's opinions are brushed aside. It was difficult to tell whether this particular test-launch of missiles by North Korea was yet another bluff in order to pressure the United States to lift the financial sanctions against it.

China's reaction began to change, however, with the continuous string of reports published in June 2006 regarding the imminent tests. For the first time, the Chinese premier openly demanded that North Korea halt its erroneous action. On 28 June 2006, Chinese Premier Wen Jiabao openly called on North Korea to stop the test-launch in an attempt to avoid Chinese domestic alarm at growing tensions in the China-North Korea relationship.[3] This reaction was unprecedented as China's senior leaders had never officially demanded anything of North Korea, even when the latter withdrew from the nuclear Non-Proliferation Treaty (NPT), reopened its 5-megawatt graphite reactor or when it declared possession of nuclear weapons in February 2005.

The reasons for China's change of position are numerous. First, it is important to note that the Chinese leadership's direct call for a halt on the missile testing came after South Korea's explicit request to China through official channels to prevent North Korea from carrying out the test launch. Since the second round of Six-Party Talks on the North Korean nuclear issue in February 2004, China and South Korea have been moving ever closer in their approach and coordination of policies. Considering South Korea's deep concern over the test launch, its direct request for Beijing to take action against this provocative move by North Korea was a request that China could not decline.

Second, China had become painfully aware of the significance of North Korea's test of a long-range missile (the *Taepodong-2*). This would be an open provocation by North Korea, after which China would have little reason to further cushion North Korea from the United States and Japan. Prior to this, China had been hoping to 'comfort' North Korea through softening the 'pressure and isolation' policy adopted by the United States and Japan and to protect North Korea from any further setback and harm. With Japan's extreme sensitivity to North Korea's missile test-launch, the firing of the new *Taepodong-2* missile would only give the United States and Japan a pretext for Japan to accelerate its cooperation with Washington in developing a ballistic missile defence capability, enhancing the US-Japan military alliance and promoting Japan's plan to intensify its military development plan. These developments would in turn complicate China's Japan policy considerably. Due to the current tension in China-Japan relations, any moves by Japan's military have the potential of stirring domestic nationalism in China that runs high with anti-Japanese sentiment. These changes in China's security environment would provide a basis for the Chinese military to demand a bigger budget and scale up its military forces. The Chinese leadership headed by Hu Jintao (China's President) does not want to see the escalation of military confrontation between China and other big powers in the region; nor does it want China's defence strategy to be manipulated by internal nationalist passions.

North Korea's missile tests have diverse implications for China. First, they show that North Korea has little regard for China's own security interests. China is deeply frustrated by North Korea's intransigent behaviour and thinking, despite five rounds of Six-Party Talks and the signing of the Joint Statement in September 2005. China had hoped that it could influence North Korea through a multilateral mechanism to create—and make routine—an exchange acceptable both to North Korea and the other parties. China's strategy in attaining these goals can be characterised as a 'soft approach', aimed at arriving at a diplomatic solution, and gradually but concretely affecting North Korea's actions. Time and again, China sternly rejected calls by the United States to increase pressure on North Korea and even took various actions to protect North Korea from further isolation. At the same time, China teamed up with South Korea, continuously providing North Korea with substantial aid, supporting South Korea's 'peace and prosperity policy' toward North Korea and respecting the requirements of Kim Jong-il for a 'security assurance' and 'fair treatment'. The *quid pro quo* of such an approach, however, was the willingness by North Korea to fully cooperate with China and South Korea, to give up its brinksmanship behaviour and to respect China's role as host of the Six-Party Talks. The launching of the missiles shows undeniably that North Korea not only lacks a basic appreciation of China's painstaking efforts on its behalf, but is showing contempt for China's security interests in Northeast Asia.

The missile tests also deeply shook the Chinese leadership's belief in the North Korean regime's ability to carry out reform and opening-up in emulation of China's model. The Chinese people also hold highly negative views of the

North Korean regime. A February 2006 public opinion poll showed that 44 per cent of Chinese people dislike North Korea more than any other country (closely following Japan, which 56 per cent of people polled most dislike). Conversely, among the three East Asian nations, South Korea is considered by the Chinese public as the country with which China most needs to deepen bilateral relations (48 per cent), followed by Japan (40 per cent), with North Korea a distant last (12 per cent).[4]

The Chinese leadership now understands it may have deluded itself about the North Korean Government. China has pursued a neighbourly policy with North Korea, thinking that it would gradually be won over by China's approach. However, the missile tests have finally revealed to the leadership in Beijing the true nature of the North Korean Government. North Korea's nuclear ambitions stem in large part from the need to safeguard its own security and interests rather than its country and people. It has also shown itself to be highly skilled in its resistance to internal reform.[5] North Korea has refused to accept China's advice and continues to take measures that intensify confrontation and defy the international community. This can only mean that the current mentality of its leaders is simplistic and arrogant. In the end, North Korea will not give serious consideration or cater to the interests of China, or take decisive steps on the road to reform and opening-up. China now objectively concedes that it is a delusion to expect the North Korean Government to make wise decisions and restart the process of merging into the world community.

Soon after the missile tests of 15 July 2006, China voted in favour of UNSC Resolution 1695 (which condemned North Korea's missile launches and imposed limited sanctions on North Korea), clearly indicating the most significant change of China's policy toward North Korea in recent years. It signifies China's growing resentment toward North Korea and implies an end to China's 'umbrella' policy for North Korea—a policy that has been in effect since the end of the Cold War and is meant to prevent the UNSC from getting entangled in North Korean affairs, and to protect North Korea from UN sanctions. With North Korea's deep dependence on China's economic and diplomatic assistance, anything that causes China to distance itself from North Korea will no doubt have implications for the survival of the Kim Government in North Korea. From the latter's perspective, China's support of the Resolution was an act of treachery by its socialist big brother. China's refusal to continue as North Korea's 'protector' in the UNSC opens the door for the possibility of new, tougher UN sanctions.

The nuclear equation: A new era

China's ire over North Korea's missile test had not yet subsided when North Korea decided to test a nuclear bomb on 9 October 2006. In Beijing, ire turned into fury. North Korea's nuclear test was a reckless violation of the September 2005 Joint Statement and squandered China's goodwill policy to accommodate

North Korea in its legitimate pursuit of security guarantees and national interest demands. The test shows that North Korea has been indifferent to China's continuous opposition and warnings against its pursuit of nuclear weapons. There is little doubt that North Korea considers its nuclear capability more important than its friendship with its only patron state, China. Without question, China has become fully disillusioned about the nature of the North Korean regime, and has come to recognise that its previous nuclear appeasement policy for North Korea must come to an end.

There is a range of speculation as to why the North Korean regime risked jettisoning China's long-term support in favour of going nuclear. Some in China argue that Kim did not believe that China would truly punish him by cutting off oil and other provisions. Certainly, North Korea is convinced that an anti-American North Korea has been a valuable strategic buffer for China vis-à-vis the US military presence in East Asia. Kim likely calculated that China would never abandon him for this reason. Others contend that Kim and his diplomats frequently hint to China that North Korea will do an 'about-face' and embrace the United States if China pushes too hard. In this way, North Korea probably believes that it holds a 'trump card' over China by playing such 'cat and mouse' tricks. However, following the nuclear test, the traditionally defined 'friendship' between the two countries evaporated. Even though China did not fully flex its muscles against North Korea, the reality is that China's resolve to dismantle the North Korean nuclear program has intensified. Its harsh words of protest over the nuclear test fully reinforce this. China called North Korea's action 'flagrant' ('*han ran*' in Chinese)—a word that is normally employed only for criticising actions by an adversary—and represents a clear break from past language by the Chinese leadership and a lucid expression of dissatisfaction and even resentment toward Kim Jong-il.

China's interest in preventing North Korea from developing nuclear weapons is fundamentally no different than the interests of both Japan and the United States. Although it is unwilling to speak with one voice alongside Tokyo and Washington in public statements, and therefore its opposition and threats toward North Korea are watered down to some extent, a North Korea with nuclear weapons is unacceptable to China.

Of primary concern, in China's judgement, is that the North Korean nuclear test has decisively shifted the nature of the problem from the 'North Korean nuclear issue', which has revolved around concerns over nuclear proliferation, to the far more dangerous and broader 'North Korean issue'. China has long tried to limit its approach with North Korea to the nuclear issue rather than the comprehensive problems—regime legitimacy, its refusal to end the Cold War on the Korean Peninsula and integrating itself into the regional community, and the unpredictability of its behaviour—fearing negative influence on China-North Korea relations and a destabilisation of the North Korean regime itself.

If North Korea fully develops and possesses nuclear weapons, fissures in the geopolitical landscape of East Asia will emerge. In the long run, this will negatively affect China's strategic interests. Since the brunt of dealing with a nuclear North Korea in the region will primarily fall to China and South Korea, they will have to strengthen their coordination efforts to this end. China simply cannot shoulder the burden alone. Closer China-South Korea cooperation could alert Japan and further drive the US-Japan military alliance. North Korea's nuclear tests might also cause Japan to accelerate its conventional military build-up and to reopen the debate in Japan on its pursuit of nuclear weapons. This will instigate a backlash in China and South Korea, further aligning the two countries while driving a bigger wedge between them and Japan. A Japan rearmed with nuclear weapons is entirely unacceptable to China, but may be welcome to the United States. This divergence of interests will lead to increased divisions between China and South Korea on one side and the United States and Japan on the other—a separation of continent states versus sea powers.

A nuclear North Korea will have its greatest direct impact on the relationship between Japan and China, and each country's domestic reactions to developments. The problem of North Korea is a double-edged sword and has the potential of either promoting or seriously harming China-Japan relations. Naturally, China's hope is that the North Korea problem will become the lubricant for better communication between the two countries. It could be a catalyst for greater discourse over regional security and cooperation. This environment probably will not lead to breakthroughs on the historical issues, but it may be a beginning in bringing the two closer. However, there is a real danger for a worsening of China-Japan ties if a spirit of cooperation is lacking and Japan's tough stand toward North Korea unsettles China. Japan also has strong nationalist sentiments against China, which will inevitably instigate a similar nationalist response from China, further engendering hostility toward one another.

As for China and the United States, while recent events are an important factor between them, their relationship also has a dynamic substantially independent of the North Korean issue. There is no question that US policy towards North Korea has been a failure and conservatives and moderates in the United States continue to be divided over China's role in the North Korean nuclear issue. As serious as it is, the side effects in solving this problem will not hugely impact the China-US relationship in the near and medium term. Nevertheless, in this context, there are many uncertainties for China's national security if force is used to resolve the North Korean nuclear issue. One great uncertainty is the future orientation of North Korea. In the past 40 years, resistance against the United States formed the basis of the China-North Korea relationship. But in 1992, by establishing diplomatic relations with South Korea, China sent a clear message that it would not support North Korea's extreme anti-US stance. This action by China was regarded by North Korea as a betrayal and its distrust still factors in the latter regime's thoughts. If China uses force to dissuade North Korean nuclear aspirations it is possible that China would not only 'lose' North Korea, but that North Korea could become anti-Chinese in nature. Most Chinese policymakers are loath to see this happen. Another uncertainty comes from America's future military presence in the Korean Peninsula. Will it decrease or increase its presence? If China and the United States can come to a consensus on North Korea, a future North Korean regime would at least not be hostile to China, alleviating one of China's concerns.

Most critical from China's perspective is to confirm whether and to what extent the United States will commit to collaborating with it in firmly yet constructively rolling back North Korea's nuclear program. Until now, Beijing has not received sufficiently clear signals from Washington on its real intention to dismantle North Korea's nuclear capability. That confirmation and trust notably revolves around issues from America's resolve to settle the issue as well as sharing in the costs and responsibilities between Beijing and Washington in any solution. One of China's greatest fears is that if China was at the forefront of any confrontation with North Korea, the United States would back down and China would be caught flatfooted and be forced to deal with North Korea on its own. China and the United States may be trapped in a dilemma where each side is unwilling to get too close to one another and act together decisively to deal with North Korea due to the logic of great power politics.[6]

Perhaps the greatest casualty of North Korea's nuclear tests has been the Six-Party Talks. Some in the United States have wanted to kick-start such a mechanism with China at the helm. However, this was always a false hope. It was never going to be realised in the medium-term or near-term without strong buttressing by others, especially the United States. As a regional security coordination mechanism, China has been carefully examining the Six-Party Talks and their potential. However, the reality is that a regional security structure evolving from the Talks is not something China can do by relying on its own strength; nor is it a mechanism in China's interests. It is not practical and is therefore no longer a policy priority for China.

Former US President George W. Bush has said that the Six-Party Talks are the best way to resolve the North Korea problem, to which Japan and South Korea have agreed as well. All are talking about a multilateral security mechanism in East Asia; however, neither the United States nor Japan nor South Korea has a feasible blueprint. Therefore, such a regional security mechanism has lost substantial attraction to China.

The current status is that the Six-Party Talks cannot reach any agreement and cannot solve the problem effectively. The Talks will not disappear in practice, though they will be in a temporary shock or paralysis. No matter where the situation goes, as long as there is any agreement in terms of North Korea's nuclear weapons, it has to be the result of a Six-Party agreement.

Internal dynamics

The question of how China's policies toward North Korea are determined is not straightforward. First of all, the current policies adopted by China are not dominated by military authorities. North Korea is now considered far less of a vital strategic 'buffer zone' than in the past. Any ultimate decision regarding China's policy toward North Korea is directly subject to judgement and selection at the highest level. Yet, the influence over that policy has always oscillated between the Ministry of Foreign Affairs (which focuses on coordination with the international community), and the International Department of the Chinese Communist Party's Central Committee (CCPCC) (which stresses the relationship between China and North Korea). While the former camp can hardly be called a 'pro-West' group, it does advocate coordination with the West. The latter camp, on the other hand, can be called 'pro-Pyongyang' and advocates strongly for cooperation with North Korea.

The CCPCC's International Department oversees exchanges with other political parties and is generally sympathetic to North Korea, often calling for a strengthened relationship between the Chinese and the North Korean political parties and governments and advocating full 'political trust' in Pyongyang. This pro-Pyongyang element also believes that, in the end, North Korea will accept China's advice to reform and open up and that China has great influence over North Korea.

Beginning with North Korea's decision to launch the missile tests, and now the nuclear tests, the International Department has had a declining influence on the formulation of Chinese policy toward North Korea. This is evidenced by a meeting held by the Central Committee on Foreign Affairs in late August 2006 which said that China would adhere to its new concept for diplomacy, including 'taking the road of peaceful development', 'opening up and mutual benefit', 'building of a harmonious world', and a 'focus on the individual'.[7] Most importantly, the conference proceedings proclaimed that a nuclear North Korea is a formidable challenge to China's 'core interests'. In Beijing's discourse, only Taiwan's independence movement has been previously interpreted in that way. The gist of these principles is that China will strengthen coordination of its own diplomacy with that of the mainstream of the international community.

The policies currently being adopted by North Korea strongly conflict with China's diplomatic goals and have greatly narrowed its space for diplomatic manoeuvring in the Six-Party Talks. It has impaired China's ability to influence the United States, Japan and others to compromise with North Korea. These difficulties, plaguing China's mediation efforts on the North Korean nuclear issue, are generating unprecedented political pressure within the Chinese Government. However, the reassessment of its North Korea policy does not automatically lead to more decisive and harsher actions against Pyongyang. It is not so easy for the Hu Jintao–Wen Jiabao team (President and Premier of China respectively) to stand up to the threat imposed by a nuclear North Korea. China is still weighing all its options and considering the most workable 'roadmap' to proceed with its policy objective of denuclearisation. Considering the delicacy and complexity of its options, Beijing will not make up its mind quickly. It is clear that a nuclear North Korea holds bleak and adverse implications for China and threatens to undermine almost all the elements of Hu Jintao's foreign policy strategy of a 'harmonious world', in which he has invested so much.[8]

The decision by the Chinese Government in May 2003 to mediate the North Korean nuclear crisis was a defining moment for Chinese diplomacy. It signalled that China would become more proactive and self-confident in its diplomatic efforts and strive to make innovative use of China's rising international influence toward playing a positive role in maintaining the country's important peripheral diplomacy. This has proven successful with the five rounds of Six-Party Talks on the North Korean nuclear issue. This is why China's participation in the Talks received extensive support in domestic mainstream public opinion. However, some academic and policy circles in China have opposed the nation's role as mediator, suggesting that China's hosting of the Six-Party Talks is tantamount to 'a small horse pulling a large cart'—that China's diplomatic clout is insufficient for the task.

In a similar vein, Hu's proactive and rational international policy approach is facing new challenges. Some in China have expressed sympathy for North Korea, believing that its actions are still a kind of support to China's strategic position and even a counter-balance to the United States and Japan.[9] Such voices grew louder following the North Korean missile launch and did not fade even after its nuclear test. Some arguments, characterised as 'conspiracy theory' (that the United States deliberately delayed the resolution on the nuclear issue with North Korea in order to reactivate Japan's rearming process) and 'transference theory' (that US intentions were to transfer more strategic pressure on China by broadening hostilities among East Asian regional members) arose to contradict the Bush Administration's moderate response and non-military intimidation against North Korea.[10] For the ossified forces within the conservative camp that were originally discontent with Hu and Wen and their new-style government, the missile launches and nuclear test only provided them with new fodder for attacking the Hu–Wen team. Chinese politics entered a sensitive period in the run up to the 17th Party Congress. North Korea's actions had, on balance, damaged the diplomatic prestige of the Chinese reformists represented by Hu and Wen. If China's policy toward North Korea is dragged into the domestic struggle over political power, the future orientation of China's diplomatic policies towards North Korea will become even more complicated.

Re-orienting China's North Korean policy

The test launch of missiles by North Korea shook Beijing's confidence in its past policy toward North Korea. The nuclear test conducted by North Korea was the last straw to substantively spur Beijing to rethink its relationship with the North.

China has implemented a range of measures in response to North Korea's defiant attitude, its missile test firing and to the negative consequences that may arise in North Korea's internal situation as a result of its actions. In terms of its overall approach, following the missile test and before the nuclear test, China began to initiate coercive diplomatic measures toward Pyongyang. This can be seen by a number of changes in China's actions toward North Korea. To begin, total trade volume between China and North Korea was reduced, especially on key products such as iron, steel, chemical and plant products. China temporarily froze an existing agreement for a large-scale development project for border trade between the two countries. An important outcome of Kim Jong-il's visit to China in January 2006 was to increase economic and trade cooperation between the border cities and regions. A large-scale border trade summit, originally scheduled for September 2006 and to be attended by high-ranking officials from both sides, was cancelled.

Meanwhile, China delayed large-scale aid measures for North Korea following the flood disaster in July 2006 and only initially provided some symbolic aid through the Red Cross. Although South Korea announced large-scale aid worth 200 billion Korean won, China stated subsequently on 30 August that 'the Chinese government is very concerned about the disaster in North Korea, and has decided to give humanitarian assistance, including grain, food, diesel and medicine', although China had yet to decide on the specific amount of goods.[11] China later decided to provide 50 000 tonnes of aid—the equivalent of half of South Korea's aid. It is a rare occurrence that China lags behind South Korea in providing disaster relief for North Korea, and it is a bellwether of China's new tendency to use economic leverage to punish the North Korean regime. As shown in Table 1 and Table 2, China-North Korea trade between July 2005 and January 2006 basically remained stagnant.

Table 1: China's Imports from North Korea from January–July 2005 to January–July 2006 ($ in US millions)

Product	January–July 2005	January–July 2006	Difference	Percentage Change
Total Value	281.626	236.687	-44.939	-15.96
Animal Products	66.616	18.055	-48.561	-72.90
Mineral Products	112.300	124.712	+12.412	+11.05
Chemical Products	0.368	0.235	-0.113	-30.71
Leather, Fur and Fur Products, Rubber	0.077	0.009	-0.068	-88.31
Wood and Wooden Products	7.124	14.112	+6.988	+98.09
Jewellery and Precious Metal	0.015	0.033	+0.018	+120.00
Basic Metal	50.413	25.942	-24.471	-48.54

Table 2: China's Exports to North Korea from January–July 2005 to January–July 2006 ($ in US millions)

Product	January–July 2005	January–July 2006	Difference	Percentage Change
Summary	618.100	678.498	+60.398	+9.77
Food, Beverages, and Tobacco	23.714	20.339	-3.375	-14.23
(Mineral Fuel, Mineral Oil, Asphalt.))	168.965	211.699	+42.73	+25.29
Fertilizer	16.482	21.618	+5.136	+31.16
Ceramics, Glass and Other Mineral Products	12.793	8.695	-4.098	-32.03
Jewellery and Precious Metal	0.067	0.043	-0.024	-35.82
Basic Metal	46.212	34.501	-11.711	-25.34
Machinery & Electronics	60.517	106.365	+45.848	+75.76

(*Source*: January–July 2006 statistics from China Customs. Its website is at <http://english.customs.gov.cn/default.aspx>, accessed 17 June 2009.)

Besides economic and aid measures, China has sent more troops to the China-North Korea border region. Although the Chinese media reported that China was sending reinforcements to the border and carrying out missile drills in the Changbai Mountains in mid-July 2006 as part of a 'routine military exercise', the fact is that China wants to enhance its ability to react in case of a contingency involving North Korea.[12] This does not represent the position of the military; rather, it indicates that China's senior leadership is very concerned about the possibility of an emergency in North Korea and has to intensify any preparation for it in the near future.

China has also tightened visa management for North Koreans entering China in an attempt to prevent North Korea from making further use of China as a conduit for illegal activities, such as smuggling and the lynching of its own citizens who try to seek sanctuary in China.

In addition, China is participating in multilateral sanctions for the first time. Furthermore, it is carrying out bilateral sanctions against North Korea. China will not obstruct strict economic sanctions and may temporarily suspend oil supplies to North Korea via the UNSC, though it would likely stop short of allowing military action against North Korea.

Yet, despite the tremendous diplomatic and political pressure exerted on China by North Korea's missile and nuclear tests, China's leaders will continue to explore the boundaries of influencing its southern neighbour. They will continue to maintain the principle of a soft approach to head off the North Korean nuclear issue. Before the North Korean nuclear test, Beijing would not have pushed its close neighbour and 'brother' into a corner, because this would not only have contravened China's own interests but also departed from the broadly accepted thinking of the Chinese people. However, if sanctions cannot move North Korea to abandon its nuclear weapons, the possibility that China will employ other means to roll back North Korea's nuclear weapons program is real. If this is the only alternative, China will use a variety of methods to accomplish that goal, including coercive diplomacy. The crucial issue here is that China will have to make a decision on how best to proceed.

How China addresses the problem of a nuclear North Korea has more to do with its resolve and less to do with its policy. Prior to the nuclear test, China saw no imperative to act decisively against North Korea: now the situation has changed dramatically. China has no alternative but to employ any and all means to get North Korea to return to its commitments to abandon nuclear weapons (exemplified in the September 2005 Joint Statement) and to map out with other parties a feasible plan to trade its nuclear capabilities for economic compensation and diplomatic normalisation. Thus, as Ambassador Wang Guangya said at the United Nations, 'no one is going to protect North Korea if it continues with its bad behaviour'.[13] China has lost its patience and its will to allow this issue to stagnate in multilateral talks. Hu Jintao presently looks to have more resolve than ever before to safeguard China against any diversion from the country's economic construction. Firmly addressing a nuclear North Korea is a big test for Hu and for China. It will add significantly to his capability and power within China and also bolster China's prestige internationally.

ENDNOTES

[1] An earlier version of this paper was published in *China Security*, Autumn 2006, pp. 35–51. It is reproduced here with the permission of the editors of *China Security*.

[2] On 24 February 2003, North Korea test-fired an anti-ship missile into the Sea of Japan; on 10 March 2003 it test-fired a second anti-ship missile into the Sea of Japan; and on 1 May 2005 it test-fired a short-range missile into the Sea of Japan. Dates and details from *Chronology of North Korean Missile Development*, Agence France-Presse, 15 June 2006, available at <http://www.spacewar.com/reports/Chronology_Of_North_Korean_Missile_Development.html>, accessed 17 June 2009. Note: This chapter was originally drafted prior to the North Korean missile tests of 2009.

[3] 'Chinese Premier Cautions North Korea on Missile Plans', *Canadian Broadcasting Corporation News*, 28 June 2006, available at <http://www.cbc.ca/world/story/2006/06/28/china-north-korea.html>, accessed 17 June 2009.

[4] Zhu Feng, 'Key Findings from 30 Chinese People: North East Asia Trialogue Survey', *China Daily*, 12 February 2006.

[5] Andrew Scobell, 'Making Sense of North Korea: Pyongyang and Comparative Communism', *Asian Security*, vol. 1, no. 3 (2005), pp. 245–66.

[6] 'Persistence on the Path of Peaceful Development and Promoting Construction of a Harmonious World', *People's Daily*, 24 August 2006, available at <http://news.xinhuanet.com/politics/2006-08/23/content_4999339.htm?rss=1>, accessed 17 June 2009.

[7] Lee Yongxie, 'The Chinese Diplomacy Advances to the World Stage', *Global Times*, 8 September 2006, available at <http://news.xinhuanet.com/world/2006-09/08/content_5063698.htm?rss=1>, accessed 17 June 2009.

[8] Dong Shandong, 'Why Punish North Korea?', Singapore Zao Bao.com, 11 July 2006, available at <http://www.zaobao.com.sg/special/forum/pages3/forum_us060711.html>, accessed 17 June 2009; Hong Zhiliang, 'Do Missiles Launched into the Sea Compare with Slaughter and Invasion?', Singapore Zao Bao.com, 10 July 2006, available at <http://www.zaobao.com.sg/special/forum/pages3/forum_jp060710.html>, accessed 17 June 2009; and 'North Korea: Realistic Grief in International Relations', Singapore Zao Bao.com, 7 August 2006, available at <http://www.zaobao.com.sg/special/forum/pages3/forum_lx060807d.html>, accessed 17 June 2009.

[9] Zhu Feng, 'Why the U.S. has Moderate Response to North Korea's Nuclear Test', *Global Times*, 1 November 2006.

[10] 'Qin Gang, Chinese Ministry of Foreign Affairs spokesperson, answers reporters' questions on Aug. 30, 2006', *Global Times*, 1 September 2006.

[11] Qiu Yongzheng, 'Who is Fabricating Rumors about the PLA?', *Elite Reference*, 6 August 2006.

[12] , 'Who is Fabricating Rumors about the PLA?', *Elite Reference*, 6 August 2006.

[13] 'S. Korea, Russia try to stop N. Korea', *Associated Press*, 5 October 2006, available at <http://cbs2.com/national/United.States.North.2.273400.html>, accessed 17 June 2009.

Chapter 6

'The Six-Party Talks Process: Towards an Asian Concert?'

Robert Ayson

The Six-Party Talks achieved an important milestone in February 2007—an agreement which required North Korea to freeze its Yongbyon reactor in exchange for some initial energy assistance and discussions on more normalised relations with the United States. North Korea was also required to come clean on all of its nuclear facilities and research by providing a complete and unabridged list.[1] But this important step was to come later rather than right at the outset. This bargain represents an important shift in the US position. Washington had earlier insisted that North Korea really had to relinquish its entire nuclear program before any concessions were granted.

Experience might suggest that North Korea got what it wanted—particularly more time when the Bush Administration was in its lame duck season—and that it has no real intention of undertaking complete nuclear disarmament. If the pessimists (or perhaps the realists) are correct, the Bush Administration took a big risk. The maximum that might be expected from North Korea could consist of the freeze, disablement and possibly removal of North Korea's facilities for producing additional weapons, but not necessarily the surrender of all elements of the existing arsenal. This suggests a de facto admission that the best that can be hoped for is the management of a reduced problem.

This risks slipping into the perspective that one simply has to learn to live with a minimally nuclear North Korea. Of the six parties, it is possible that China, Russia and South Korea are relatively comfortable with that prospect (and some in Washington may even be willing to do so as well). Perhaps disarmament is simply not a pragmatic option—as long as North Korea acts within reasonable bounds and is not an embarrassment for its neighbours, is some sort of nuclear capability tolerable? But this would still be quite a sacrifice for China. It means giving up on being the only North Asian state with nuclear weapons. Moreover, even a very small yet frozen North Korea nuclear arsenal would prove an all too easy basis on which Japan could justify its missile defence programs, and indeed perhaps take even more adventurous steps. These are not outcomes which China would want to see encouraged.

The Six-Party Talks process will continue to be challenging. Early steps were stalled by painstaking negotiations to release North Korean funds deposited into a Macau-based financial house. Lingering concerns about North Korea's interest in uranium enrichment (as well as its traditional route of plutonium extraction) will haunt future developments. Any list that North Korea produces is unlikely to gain universal confidence. The process has been very demanding on the patience of its main participants. This includes China, which is not only the host of the talks but is also commonly viewed as the country with the greatest leverage over North Korea—a supposed advantage which also encourages unrealistic expectations about what Beijing may be able to get Pyongyang to do. It also includes the United States whose former envoy, Christopher Hill, showed the patience of Job.

Measuring the Six-Party Talks properly

North Korea may be willing to have the vast majority of its production capacities removed for the right price. But giving up all semblance of nuclear weapons status is a different prospect. It remains unlikely that the Six-Party Talks will result in the complete removal of all traces of North Korea's nuclear weapons, but it is not clear that this is the benchmark against which the success of the Talks should be judged. When assessed against more modest objectives for the North Korean situation and wider objectives North Asia, the Six-Party Talks process offers some distinct advantages.

First, the Talks have provided a mechanism short of the use of force for dealing with North Korea. The response to North Korea's nuclear test in late 2006 was not a military attack. It was sustained pressure (including the coercive power of an attack option left on the table and intensive encouragement from China) which led to a resumption of the Six-Party Talks in early 2007 and the February agreement mentioned at the start of this chapter. Like all multilateral processes involving exhaustive discussions which for years can go nowhere, the Six-Party Talks process has had plenty of critics. But few, if any, of its detractors have come up with a better approach to addressing North Korea's nuclear weapons program. The Six-Party Talks is one of those processes (like the Asia-Pacific Economic Cooperation (APEC) in the early 1990s) that would need to be invented if it was not already available. In other words, it is better to judge the efficacy of the Six-Party Talks against the uncertain and incomplete outcomes which non-existent or non-effective alternatives might provide rather than against some absolutist but fantastical goal of complete North Korean nuclear disarmament. In dealing with North Korea, as the author has argued elsewhere, the least ugly option is king.[2]

Second, through the Six-Party Talks process North Korea has been held in a loose but multilateral embrace of five significant regional powers. Differences certainly remain between them in their positions. Japan is the unhappiest. Its refusal to provide financial assistance to North Korea until Pyongyang addresses the outstanding abductee issue is rather like asking for a 30-minute start in the Olympic marathon: it simply will not happen. But Japan genuinely feels that a nuclear North Korea—its near neighbour under whose missile shadow it falls—is getting too good a deal.[3] This has opened up some tensions between Japan and the United States, which views North Korea as a proliferation risk on the other side of the Pacific Ocean. And China continues to see North Korea as a domestic instability risk across the border. There is no doubt that different motivations are in play here.

Yet, through the Six-Party Talks process, these three largest powers in East Asian security affairs—the United States, China and Japan—have been required to explore and negotiate the differences in their policies towards an urgent regional security issue. Their policy convergence is certainly incomplete. They do not always agree and the Six-Party Talks process may end up with a result that none of them are entirely satisfied with. But they have found enough common interests to remain part of the process despite the difficulty of dealing with North Korea. If the Six-Party Talks can be a modest way of encouraging great power cooperation in Asia, it will have been worth the effort. This means that even if the final impact of the Talks process on the North Korean nuclear weapons program is less than decisive, it may have done something even more important for Asia. What is special about the Six-Party Talks is not that it is focused on the North Korean nuclear situation per se. The Talks process is special because all of the major powers in East Asia are sitting around the table working on an important security issue.[4]

Inclusive and exclusive alternatives

This incipient but focused collaboration between Asia's major powers is rare. This is not to suggest that the Six-Party Talks process is the only forum in the Asia-Pacific that includes 'the big three'. APEC offers the potential for great power get-togethers on its sidelines among the region's leaders, but seems generally more sympathetic to US and Western views than to those of East Asia. It has a very broad membership which means that, while it includes the great powers, it also has to incorporate the small ones whose roles in the Asian power equation are always going to be modest. It is probably not the ideal forum for managing the security challenges of North Asia over the long-term. Its agenda, official or informal, does not seem likely to be easily harnessed or available for direct work on the issues that affect direct relations between the big powers in North Asia. APEC's main security outcomes so far—as a platform for the East Timor intervention in 1999 and more recently in encouraging regional counter-terrorism and counter-pandemic cooperation—are side issues to the great power balance.

The ASEAN Regional Forum (ARF) is also too inclusive and is hamstrung by its lowest common denominator ethos. Smaller powers, including its hosts, are inclined to advance their interests in being recognised as the official drivers of Asian multilateralism and their own sub-regional preoccupations, ahead of deep and meaningful contact directly between the great powers of North Asia. Some years ago the founding members of ASEAN created something very close to a Southeast Asian security community based on the norm that states in the community should avoid conflict with one another. This stands as a remarkable achievement. But the idea of spreading this sometimes patchy normative framework to the rest of Asia through ASEAN-centred processes looks much better in theory than in practice.

APEC and the ARF are two of the more established regional fora and have been supplemented by new ones. But the newer kids on the block—ASEAN Plus Three (APT) and the East Asia Summit (EAS)—are unlikely to be concerts in the making because both exclude the United States. And, rather than serving as locations for cooperation between their two great power members from East Asia (China and Japan), they have become venues for their competition for influence over the rest of the region. For now, at least, Japan's favourite, the EAS (which includes the balancing presence of Australia, New Zealand and India), is running second to the more important—and ironically more East Asian—APT, which is China's favoured mechanism. This may seem beneficial for China's interests in the short term, but an approach which keeps the United States out and Japan down is not likely to be good for the great power stability in Asia on which China also depends.

An embryonic concert?

By comparison, while the Six-Party Talks process is by no means a perfect arrangement, it may offer the best chance as a bridge to an Asian 'concert of powers'. This concert would not be a permanent, formal, institution.[5] Instead, it would be a process of great power collaboration which creates such stabilising and convergent expectations that, when major problems arise, the major powers can sit down together and seek to manage their differences. If it is anything like the European concert of the early nineteenth century, an Asian concert would be highly discriminatory. Only the biggest powers would need to apply for membership (in fact they would appoint themselves in a process of self-selection). The interests of the smaller powers (the non-members of the concert) could get overlooked. But if the small and medium powers of the region (like Australia, New Zealand and the ASEAN countries) also depend on stable relations between the great powers for the future of Asian security, and if those stable relations are only really achievable if the great powers can sit down and work out their differences with one another, then some sacrifice of the one-state, one-vote principle may be in order.

Of course, not all the members of the Six-Party Talks process may themselves belong in that concert. Neither South Korea nor North Korea really qualifies as a great power. Six parties minus two leaves four. Russia's hydrocarbon-induced return to bully power status under Vladimir Putin might not have been as deeply established as some feared, and was aimed much more at European than Asian influence. Four parties minus one leaves three. Most certainly the United States and China belong to the concert. After all, it is their relationship that Asia's future security order depends on most of all. Japan's place is a little less certain. It is not a great power in terms of possessing a permanent seat at the United Nations Security Council (UNSC), in terms of possessing nuclear weapons, or in terms of the constitutional restrictions on the deployment of Japan's military. But Japan needs to be part of the concert simply because China-Japan and US-Japan relations are the other legs of that vital tripod in North Asia. There is also a need, at least eventually, to include a fourth great power in the concert. This is India—Asia's second rising great power. This confirms that, while the Talks may contribute to the Concert, the Concert is not the Six-Party Talks.

A concert of Asia-Pacific powers—which seeks to extend the limited cooperation that has been seen at the Six-Party Talks—might well prove ineffective because of the difference in strategic interests between its members. It would include the three leading relationships of strategic competition in Asia: in the near-term between China and Japan; in the medium-term between China and the United States; and in the long-term between China and India. But even an ineffective great power concert could be preferable to the strengthening of rival and mutually exclusive groupings in Asia which might split the region into conflicting blocs.

A clash of alliances

One of these blocs could emerge as an alliance of maritime democracies under US leadership. The clearest form of this idea has actually been presented by Japan: the Asian democratic quad favoured during Japanese Prime Minister Shinzo Abe's brief premiership, which would add Australia and India to the mix. This is not to say that all elements of closer cooperation between any of these four powers form a necessary pathway to that quad. But they could do so. The debate over Australia's new security declaration with Japan is a case in point. Championed by Abe and Australia's former Prime Minister, John Howard, the declaration received only cautious support from Howard's political rival Kevin Rudd (now Australian Prime Minister), who warned against any moves to take the relationship down the alliance path.[6] Likewise Rudd argued that his support for the increasingly close Trilateral Strategic Dialogue between the United States, Japan and Australia did not mean an endorsement of any attempts to encircle China. This is an important point because, for some observers, the emergence of a de facto (if not de jure) trilateral alliance between the United

States and its two leading alliance partners in Asia—Japan and Australia—may be an idea whose time has come.

Many of the arguments against a full quad of Asian democracies are practical ones. Quite simply, India wishes to retain its foreign policy autonomy. While New Delhi welcomes the chance to enjoy closer security relations with the United States, Japan and Australia, its preference is for a series of bilateral relationships. It wants to stay out of the quad. Australia is also reluctant. But representatives from the four countries did meet together in early 2007 on the sidelines of an ARF meeting in the Philippines, and China revealed its discomfort by sending a diplomatic note of concern to each of the four capitals.[7]

China has access to a potential response to this maritime alliance in the form of the Shanghai Cooperation Organisation (SCO), which could be the basis for an alliance of continental autocracies in which Russia also plays a leading role, and to which countries like Iran and North Korea might well be attracted. Large scale 'anti-terrorism' exercises conducted under SCO auspices may well be an early sign of competition with the recent emergence of trilateral and quadrilateral exercises involving the maritime powers in Asia.

There is a small amount of overlap between the groupings. For example, India is an observer of the SCO—a clear sign of its position as a swing state in Asia. Yet, for the most part, the groupings are mutually exclusive. For example, the alliance of democracies would be based on many shared interests and values between its members. But it would, by definition, automatically exclude China.

These two blocs would each be stronger than the more diverse and unwieldy great power concert. The blocs would be more effective in pursuing their own objectives. But they could divide the region so that the Asia of 2014 would look too much like the Europe of 1914 and we all know what happens next. Against this prospect, the Six-Party Talks process carries the hint of a more promising future. Not a perfect Asia where all differences between the great powers are resolved. Not a complete answer to the security problems that the concert would undoubtedly struggle with. But a partially successful alternative to the dangerous two-horse race which could emerge between blocs led by China and the United States.

Conclusion

A great power concert in Asia, however ineffective, is preferable to an Asia dangerously divided between two rival blocs, however internally effective these blocs may be. But for a flawed but still valuable concert to operate, almost all of the participating countries would have to give up something. In other words, in order to win, one would have to lose. Let us look first at the great powers. The United States has to give up the idea that it can maintain primacy in Asia. A great power concert means that the United States will have to share hegemony, including with China. It will need to soften its emphasis on a network of military alliances with other maritime democracies in the region.

China probably has rather less to lose, but it still has to relinquish something. It will need to abandon any ideas that it will be the single leader of Asia. Unlike the SCO, of which Beijing is the natural leader, a great power concert means that China will need to share power, and not just with the United States but with India, and, hardest of all, with Japan as well. This means recognising Tokyo's right to a seat at the big table.

But Japan may itself have a lot to lose in a concert. An alliance of democracies would be a big win for Japan, providing Tokyo with significant status and an unprecedented chance to boost its role in regional security affairs and to work alongside other democracies which want to see Japan play that bigger role. But, in the concert, Japan will have continually to regulate its diplomacy with China sitting across the table. This will help manage the development of its new international personality in a way that Japan will sometimes find uncomfortable.

Some of the smaller and medium powers in the region may have even more to lose from a concert—at least in the short term. Australia is simply not big enough to qualify for a seat at the really big table that a great power concert would involve. By some calculations of Australia's short-term diplomatic interests, this can make the alliance of democracies attractive as a way of boosting Australia's profile. But, in the long-term, that alliance would encourage a hostile division between the United States and China and between Japan and China. This would run counter to Australia's interests in making sure that the China-US balance does not turn ugly, and that a major conflict between China and Japan is also avoided. For that reason, a concert which includes all three of these giants, as well as India, is in Australia's long-term strategic interests. But this would probably mean a less prominent role for Australia in some of the important diplomacy of the region.

Australia still has an important role to play, often behind the scenes. China regards Australia as a strategic economic partner. The United States regards Australia as one of the closest allies it has anywhere in the world. And Japan regards Australia as an emerging security partner. With those sorts of linkages, Australia can encourage these three powers to seek the Asian concert which involves them all, however shaky and ineffective this may turn out to be. And this means continuing to support the Six-Party Talks process, even if it does not lead to a completely denuclearised North Korea. (Had the Talks dealt with North Korea's nuclear weapons issue quickly, its full potential as a bridge to an Asian concert might well have been overlooked.) Canberra regards the freezing and disablement of North Korea's nuclear weapons program as important outcomes to work towards. But the possibility of great power collaboration over the longer term in Asia, with the Six-Party Talks acting an important step along the way, is, in this author's opinion, the more important prize.

ENDNOTES

[1] See Ministry of Foreign Affairs of the People's Republic of China, 'Initial Actions for the Implementation of the Joint Statement', 13 February 2007, available at <http://www.fmprc.gov.cn/eng/zxxx/t297463.htm>, accessed 17 June 2009.

[2] See Robert Ayson and Brendan Taylor, 'Attacking North Korea: Why War Might be Preferred', *Comparative Strategy*, vol. 23, no. 3, July–September 2004, pp. 263–79.

[3] For a more recent account, see Michael Green and James J. Przystup, 'The Abductee Issue is a Test of America's Strategic Credibility', *PacNet*, no. 47, Pacific Forum-CSIS, Honolulu, 15 November 2007.

[4] For a much less positive assessment, see Mitchell Reiss, 'A Nuclear-Armed North Korea: Accepting the 'Unacceptable'?', *Survival*, vol. 48, no. 4, Winter 2006–07, pp. 97–109.

[5] See Carsten Holbraad, *The Concert of Europe: A Study in German and British International Theory 1815-1914*, Longman, London, 1970, p. 2.

[6] See Kevin Rudd, 'A Federal Labor Government Would Enhance Australia's Security Relationship with Japan', Media Statement, 7 March 2007.

[7] See 'China demarches to 4 nations', *The Hindu*, 14 June 2006, available at <http://www.thehindu.com/2007/06/14/stories/2007061404451200.htm>, accessed 17 June 2009.

Chapter 7

The US Role in the Future Security Architecture for East Asia

Ron Huisken

Although the US role in East Asia over the period 1900–45 was by no means inconsequential, this investigation will take up the story from 1945. Washington approached the questions of post-war arrangements in Europe and East Asia with one big lesson from the First World War in mind: that staying engaged and shaping the course of events directly was smarter than walking away and trusting the local powers to preclude history repeating itself. In Europe, even though the United States had a decisive voice after the defeat of Nazi Germany, the winners' side of the table was pretty crowded with the likes of the United Kingdom, France and the Soviet Union. In East Asia, the United States had a freer hand, and the success of the Manhattan Project allowed the defeat of Japan to be accelerated sufficiently to make the bargains struck at Potsdam in June 1945 regarding Soviet participation in ending the war in the Pacific all but redundant.

At the same time, East Asia did not compare with Europe as a region that had and should continue to engage US interests comprehensively. Japan was both an enemy (vanquished, but to be kept down) and the only state in a vast region that had any pedigree as an advanced, industrial power and thus the potential to be a profitable economic and, imaginably, political partner for the United States. Moreover, despite an abundance of signs that relations with the Soviet Union were going to be a defining difficulty of the post-war period, the United States de-mobilised quite extravagantly in the years 1945–49 and resisted the notion that a new 'war' was already underway which would require it to maintain substantial armed forces on a permanent basis. These inhibitions were abandoned with the formation of the North Atlantic Treaty Organization (NATO) in April 1949. The Soviet nuclear test in August 1949 and US President Harry S. Truman's decision to develop the hydrogen bomb a few months later confirmed that there would be no re-consideration or turning back. Truman also commissioned the preparation of a study of what a Cold War with, and containment of, the Soviet Union would imply for the military capabilities the United States would have to regard as 'normal' even in peacetime. This study, *United States Objectives and Programs for National Security* (NSC-68), was completed in April 1950 and recommended full-scale development of the nuclear forces alongside the comprehensive re-development of US conventional forces. But, in the absence of a clear political trigger to justify re-armament, NSC-68 languished.

East Asia, of course, ranked a poor second to Europe. The communist victory in China's civil war appears to have been regarded in Washington, at least initially, more as a disappointment than a strategic reversal. Similarly, China's early occupation of Taiwan to complete the process was anticipated and accepted. The United States was disillusioned with its local partners in the southern half of Korea and began withdrawing its forces in 1949. These several straws came together in a now-famous speech by US Secretary of State Allen Dulles in January 1950 which implied only too clearly that the United States saw its vital interests in Northeast Asia as limited to the Japanese islands. A few months later, in June 1950, the United States nonetheless promptly decided to contest North Korea's Soviet-enabled invasion of South Korea, to endorse NSC-68 as an initial blueprint for a characteristically spectacular re-armament program (the Pentagon budget went up more than three-fold in real terms between 1950 and 1953), and, on the second day of the war, 26 June 1950, to view China's expected invasion of Taiwan as an unhelpful complication that should be deterred by deploying the 7th Fleet to the Taiwan Strait. At the time, China had no known association with the invasion, and disguised its infiltration of volunteers during October and November 1950 until the last possible moment. This prompt sealing-off of Taiwan suggests that, in the early months of 1950, the United States had become at least ambivalent about what it would do if China moved against the island.

The United States had toyed with a Pacific counterpart to NATO, but this only made sense to the United States if Japan was included while Japan's inclusion deterred every other interested party. America's appetite for additional 'entangling alliances', especially in theatres of secondary importance, faded until the Korean War revived the imperatives needed to overcome these domestic hesitations. America's military footprint in East Asia can therefore be said to have been supported in a rather general sense by the drift toward the Cold War and the resolve to posture itself to 'contain' Soviet expansion during the late 1940s, but with the specifics driven by the imperatives of the Korean War: larger forces permanently deployed in Japan, the new commitments to the defence of South Korea and Taiwan and codified bilateral security arrangements with the Philippines, Thailand and Australia/New Zealand—the so-called 'hubs and spokes' pattern of alliances rather than a single collective security pact along the lines of NATO. Apart from the changed arrangements with Taiwan, including the withdrawal of all US forces, following US-China re-engagement in 1972, this US military presence in East Asia remained unchanged for 50 years.

The American purpose in committing itself to the indefinite forward-deployment of significant military capabilities was to preclude the use or threat of use of force to change boundaries, to as far as possible deny the Soviet Union and China any soft options for the spread of communism, and to reassure itself and the wider region that Japanese militarism was a thing of the past. An additional driver, prominent in the preceding century but much less so in the early years after the Second World War, was that a generally stable region would be hospitable to US trade and investment. Over time, as the Japanese economic miracle of 1955–70 sparked comparable phases of dramatic growth in South Korea, Hong Kong, Taiwan, Singapore and other ASEAN states, most elites in Asia subscribed to the view that there was a powerful association between the US military presence and East Asia's strategic tranquility on the one hand and the region's transforming economic dynamism on the other hand. Not even the trauma of the Vietnam War seemed to dent this view. Indeed, most seem to subscribe to former Singaporean Prime Minister Lee Kuan Yew's assessment that the Vietnam War bought an additional decade for the new non-communist states of Asia to build their economic and political resilience. Unsurprisingly, official US justifications for sustaining their forward presence in Asia, directed equally at domestic and foreign audiences, began to refer more prominently to this presence as the 'oxygen' that sustained growth and development.

The end of the Cold War in 1989–91 naturally rocked the foundations of this US-dominated security system in East Asia. Washington reacted first (but under strident public pressure), moving unilaterally to declare that the new circumstances allowed the US Administration to initiate a significant drawdown in US forces stationed abroad in Europe and Asia, but without stepping back from the security obligations that these forces were intended to meet. In other words, the United States wanted to (and thought it safely could) thin-out its forward-deployed forces without signalling any basic transformation of its global security posture. East Asians apparently thought otherwise, viewing the drawdown alongside America's withdrawal from its large bases in the Philippines as potentially destabilising. The signals of discomfort and concern received in the United States were such that the drawdown was terminated well short of the target, and the United States Government set out to reassure Asian audiences that it would keep 100 000 US military personnel forward-deployed in Asia into the indefinite future. Even so, Washington found that fully repairing the loss of confidence in its resolve to underwrite regional security took several years.

Less visibly, an entirely different policy response to the end of the Cold War was taking shape in the Pentagon. The then Secretary of Defense, Dick Cheney, was in the market for a new grand strategy—some coherent set of ideas that could replace the Soviet Union as guidance for US foreign and security policy settings in place of what he saw as a rather aimless and potentially dangerous dissipation of US power.

It is important to note, first of all, that the central thesis of the Pentagon strategy was not the literal adoption of a particular strand of obscure academic thinking. It would seem that the foundations for the strategy were built up rather pragmatically—'discovered' as Cheney put it—by officials of the neo-conservative persuasion in response to the challenge of defending the Pentagon's budget from the pressures for a post Cold War peace dividend. An influential consideration in crafting this strategy was that the United States had endured some major scares during the Cold War and should at all costs avoid the emergence of another 'peer competitor'. Given the opportunity to build a new order, the first requirement was to avoid getting back into a glass jar with another scorpion (the classic depiction of the United States and the Soviet Union in circumstances of mutual assured destruction). The obvious precursor to a global rival was the emergence of a regional hegemon where the resources of the hegemon and its immediate region provided the strategic muscle to challenge the United States globally. This, too, had to be prevented. Regions like Africa and Latin America could be ruled out with reasonable confidence as a springboard for global rivalry with the United States, but Europe, the Middle East and East Asia were another matter.

The neo-conservative prescription differed significantly from that of the Realists—the mainstream school of thought about these matters. Realists contended that the US propensity toward idealism and messianism had to be held in check by a rigorous focus on 'national interests'. The policy prescription from this school was to guard against the risk that winning the Cold War would encourage the view that the United States—the state that was the exception to all other hegemonic powers the world had ever experienced—was now free to reshape the world to its advantage, and that doing so would be recognised by all (or nearly all) as to their benefit as well. Realists favoured the discipline of recognising the limits of US power and confining the nation's foreign policy ambitions to the protection and advancement of rigorously defined national interests.[1]

The draft Pentagon strategy called for the United States to be the dominant outside power in the Middle East and Persian Gulf regions to protect access to oil. In Europe and Asia, the United States would seek to prevent any of the resident major powers from dominating the region and perhaps using the consolidated resources of the region as a springboard to global power status. On Weapons of Mass Destruction (WMD), the draft noted that 'the United States could be faced with the question of whether to take military steps to prevent the development or use of weapons of mass destruction'—a rather clear indication that pre-emption could emerge as the preferred or necessary option.

The draft went a crucial step further: it suggested that the United States should actively discourage the emergence of potentially competitive powers, and pointed to several policy settings that would contribute to this objective. Specifically:

> First, the United States must show the leadership necessary to establish and protect a new order that holds the promise of convincing potential competitors that they need not aspire to a greater role or pursue a more aggressive posture to protect their legitimate interests. Second, in the non-defense areas, we must account sufficiently for the interests of the advanced industrial nations to discourage them from challenging our leadership or seeking to overturn the established political and economic order. Finally, we must maintain the mechanisms for deterring potential competitors from even aspiring to a larger regional or global role. An effective reconstitution capability is important here, since it implies that a potential rival could not hope to quickly or easily gain a predominant military position in the world.[2]

These thoughts went to the heart of the brief. They mandated a militarily dominant United States capable of acting independently when collective action could not be orchestrated and visibly positioned to increase its military power faster than any potential competitor. Cheney considered these strands of thinking to be a promising step toward a strategy that would be politically viable and would protect US military superiority.

This strategy would commit the United States to a very demanding and costly international role into the indefinite future, something that the American public was seeking to get away from. Strangely, however, no other groups in the foreign and security policy community in Washington had yet even been exposed to it, let alone persuaded of its merits. In other words, there had been no whole-of-government assessment and review. In fact, the Pentagon strategy ran counter to sentiments elsewhere in the US Administration, particularly in the White House, and may even have been intended to contest these sentiments. For example, US President George H.W. Bush's *National Security Strategy* of August 1991 said:

> If the end of the Cold War lives up to its promise and liberates U.S. policy from many of its earlier concerns, we should be able to concentrate more on enhancing security—in the developing world, particularly through means that are more political, social and economic than military.
>
> ...
>
> In the face of competing fiscal demands and a changing but still dangerous world, we have developed a new defense strategy that provides the conceptual framework for our future forces. This new strategy will guide our deliberate reductions *to no more than the forces we need to defend our interests and meet our global responsibilities.*[3]

When a copy of the Pentagon document was leaked to the *New York Times* in March 1992, its thesis was savaged from all sides, and it was disowned by Bush. A new draft, appropriately softer in tone and giving new prominence to the importance of allies and the United Nations, was also 'leaked' (in May 1992) without reviving the controversy. After this, as the Presidential election campaign of 1992 intensified, the issue seemed to disappear.

We now know, however, that Cheney tasked Lewis 'Scooter' Libby (then assistant to the then US Undersecretary of Defense Paul Wolfowitz) to further develop the basic ideas of the strategy.[4] Libby endorsed the core proposition that US military superiority should be so stark and overwhelming that no other state would even consider setting out on the long road to challenge it, but he added that this superiority should be extant rather than dependent on a reconstitution capability. In this way, unipolarity, at least in the military dimension, would remain a permanent feature of the international landscape.

In the last days of the George H.W. Bush Administration (that is, in January 1993), Cheney issued a document called *Defense Strategy for the 1990s: The Regional Defense Strategy*.[5] Journalists learned later that this was in fact a sanitised version of the Pentagon strategy. It is instructive, therefore, to take a closer look at this statement.

Cheney's defence strategy was an eminently marketable product, presenting a relatively optimistic view of the security outlook and highlighting allies (frequently) as a critical strategic asset for the United States. Its network of alliances constituted a 'zone of peace' and a 'framework for security not through competitive rivalry in arms, but through cooperative approaches and collective security institutions'.[6]

Several interesting themes permeated the document. One was the notion that the end of the Cold War had given the United States greater 'strategic depth'. This outcome, which took as given the fact that the United States was militarily dominant in every region that mattered, resulted from two factors. First, the Soviet Union was no longer there to boost the military potential of regional actors threatening US interests. Second, absent the pervasive ideological contest with the Soviet Union and the Cold War concern that even peripheral Soviet gains could begin to tip the central balance, the United States no longer had to spread its resources to cover every front. It now had greater choice about where it should focus its energy. A third factor might be regarded as implicit in these two, but is worth drawing out. The demise of the Soviet Union not only greatly enhanced America's relative power; it also made it much safer for the United States to exercise that power. During the Cold War, any clash of US and Soviet armed forces carried an irreducible risk of escalation to strategic nuclear war. This inhibiting risk was now gone. Cheney's document stressed that this relatively luxurious position had been won at great cost and should therefore not be 'squandered'.

A second theme Cheney stressed was that allied support was most effectively assured if it was clear that the United States had the ability, and the will, to win by itself if necessary. History, the document plausibly argued, 'suggests that effective multilateral action is most likely to come about in response to US leadership, not as an alternative to it'.[7] Preserving the ability to act independently was essential insurance, and responded to the lessons of history. Later, and with considerable prescience, the document addressed possible domestic impediments to the role it recommended the United States play. Specifically, Cheney's document argued that the security challenges of the future would not be the major, global, relatively 'black and white' contests that the American public could be relied upon to support. On the contrary, US interests in regional conflicts 'may seem less apparent' and US involvement rather more optional. To counter the risk that future administrations may find it difficult to generate or sustain public support for military ventures in distant places, the United States needed the capacity to respond decisively to regional crises, 'to win quickly and with minimum casualties'.

The document did not repeat the proposal that the United States should actively discourage the emergence of rival powers, but it came close:

> It is not in our interest or those of the other democracies to return to earlier periods in which multiple military powers balanced against one another in what passed for security structures, while regional, or even global peace hung in the balance.
>
> ...
>
> Our fundamental belief in democracy and human rights gives other nations confidence that our significant military power threatens no one's aspirations for peaceful democratic progress.[8]

Other language in the document betrayed a deep appreciation of the political options that flowed from America's emergence from the Cold War as a military colossus. The notion of shaping security environments is a very old one. It refers to activities, including military activities, designed to discourage and deter developments deemed injurious to the national interest. Cheney's document, however, goes a significant step further to suggest, throughout, that the US objective should be to *preclude* (that is, make impossible) regional threats and challenges, or hostile non-democratic powers from dominating regions of importance to the United States. This posture, the document states, 'is not simply within our means: it is critical to our future security'.[9] Many analysts would see in this observation evidence of the propensity in hegemonic states toward strategic over-reach; that is, toward the adoption of postures that almost ensure the eventual exhaustion of the capacity or the collapse of the political will needed to sustain them.

The Pentagon strategy essentially disappeared from view for nearly a decade; that is, for the two terms of the Clinton Administration, for the Bush/Gore election campaign in 2000, and, so it seemed, for the first 18 months of the George W. Bush Administration. Eventually, in June 2002, Bush quite abruptly declared the Pentagon strategy to be the policy of the United States, using the starkest formulations of its key premises. Speaking at the West Point military academy on 1 June 2002, Bush said:

> As we defend the peace, we also have an historic opportunity to preserve the peace. We have our best chance since the rise of the nation state in the 17th century to build a world where the great powers compete in peace instead of prepare for war. The history of the last century, in particular, was dominated by a series of destructive national rivalries that left battlefields and graveyards across the Earth. Germany fought France, the Axis fought the Allies, and then the East fought the West, in proxy wars and tense standoffs, against a backdrop of nuclear Armageddon.
>
> Competition between great nations is inevitable, but armed conflict in our world is not. More and more, civilized nations find ourselves on the same side—united by common dangers of terrorist violence and chaos. America has, and intends to keep, military strengths beyond challenge, thereby making the destabilizing arms races of other eras pointless, and limiting rivalries to trade and other pursuits of peace.[10]

Several facets of the Pentagon strategy are of particular interest. First, in advocating that the US step forward and declare its intention to take charge, and to ensure that its leadership could not be challenged, the strategy departed from a posture that US Administrations had consistently preferred for over a century. Second, the strategy had been wholly crafted within the Pentagon and had never been subjected to the usual inter-agency review and assessment. Third, the strategy never formed the basis of anyone's political platform and was therefore never tested electorally. In mid-2002, with the enduring shock of the 11 September 2001 terrorist attacks on the United States, the 'axis of evil', the doctrine of pre-emption and the political manoeuvring over regime change in Iraq, the announcement made little impact. In the circumstances, it seemed all but redundant. Still, enough of the senior leadership in the Bush Administration attached importance to seeing it adopted as a formal policy setting. It is true, of course, that Bush won a second term in 2004 (what he has described as an 'accountability moment' for his policies), but it seems fair to say that the Pentagon's 'grand strategy' was so completely sidelined by Iraq and the global 'war on terror' that it had no visibility with the electorate.

The Clinton Administration, as could be inferred from its election slogan '*It's the economy, stupid*', shared the instincts of its predecessor and opted for caution in the realm of foreign and security policy. Its 'bottom up' review of the US defence posture identified the Korean Peninsula and the Persian Gulf as the two most testing security challenges that could arise, particularly if they erupted at about the same time. Thus, coping with two medium regional conflicts (2MRC) occurring in overlapping timeframes became the benchmark against which the Pentagon measured the adequacy of its capabilities. Other challenges, especially terrorism, the proliferation of WMD and the characteristic of asymmetry inherent in these phenomena received a prominent mention, but were basically subsumed in the more traditional 2MRC mission. Moreover, this mission basically validated the forward-deployments that had emerged from the Cold War.

The eight years of Bill Clinton's presidency witnessed an increasingly heated debate about the scope for the information revolution and capacities for long-range precision strike, in particular, to transform the conduct of conventional warfare, especially if there was the courage to not only acquire the technologies but to explore the capacity of radically different military formations, command and control arrangements, and arrangements for the collection and dissemination of intelligence to capture the full synergistic potential of these new technologies. Although the pile of major studies pointing to the possibility that the United States could 'transform' conventional war and place itself far ahead of all potential rivals grew higher throughout the 1990s, the Clinton Administration saw no compelling reason to rush into this new era. The Pentagon's 1998 *East Asian Strategy Report* observed that while

> this transformation involves harnessing new technologies, operational concepts and organizational structures to give U.S. forces greater mobility, flexibility and military capabilities so that they can dominate any future battlefield, the administration judged that the improvements in military hardware and support systems are not yet at the stage of fundamentally altering our strategic perceptions or force structure in the region, or elsewhere around the world.[11]

The stridency of the debate, and the progressive breakdown of bipartisanship even on national security, was reflected in the decision of the US Congress to establish a National Defense Panel (NDP) to critique the Administration's *Quadrennial Defense Review* of 1997. The NDP castigated the 2MRC as precluding the acquisition of capabilities within reach and important to coping with the different security challenges taking shape: mobility, stealth, speed, increased range, precision strike, and a smaller logistical footprint. Part of the US Administration's caution stemmed from the view that the US military had to remain ready at all times to defeat large-scale trans-border aggression by a significant military power or coalition. For many, however, including the authors of the NDP, available technologies had already transformed the nature of war such that the United States no longer had to think in terms of massive, force-on-force engagements even for the largest imaginable military threats.

The Clinton Administration, in opting to defer full-scale exploration of these possibilities, also refined its thinking about how America's extant military posture, particularly in Asia, effectively advanced US interests. *The United States Security Strategy for the East Asia-Pacific Region, 1998*, is worth quoting in full on this score:

> U.S. military presence in Asia has long provided critical and symbolic contributions to regional security. Our forces stationed in Japan and Korea, as well as those rotated throughout the region, promote security and stability, deter conflict, give substance to our security commitments and ensure our continued access to the region.
>
> Our military presence in Asia serves as an important deterrent to aggression, often lessening the need for a more substantial and costly U.S. response later. Today deterrent capability remains critical in areas such as the Korean Peninsula. A visible U.S. force presence in Asia demonstrates firm determination to defend U.S., allied and friendly interests in this critical region.
>
> In addition to its deterrent function, U.S. military presence in Asia serves to shape the security environment to prevent challenges from emerging at all. U.S. force presence mitigates the impact of historical regional tensions and allows the United States to anticipate problems, manage potential threats and encourage peaceful resolution of disputes. Only through active engagement can the United States contribute to constructive political, economic and military development within Asia's diverse environment. Forward presence allows the United States to continue playing a role in broadening regional confidence, promoting democratic values and enhancing common security.
>
> Overseas military presence also provides political leaders and commanders the ability to respond rapidly to crises with a flexible array of options. Such missions may include regional and extra-regional contingencies, from humanitarian relief, non-combatant evacuation and peacekeeping operations to meeting active threats as in the Arabian Gulf. During the Arabian Gulf crisis in early 1998, for example, USS *Independence* deployed to the Gulf and was an important element of our deterrent force posture that alleviated the crisis. Military presence also enhances coalition operations by promoting joint, bilateral and combined training, and encouraging responsibility sharing on the part of friends and allies.[12]

In a speech in February 2001, former US President George W. Bush declared that the United States would aspire to keep the peace by *redefining war on its terms*. He did so in the context of announcing that he had given the then US Secretary of Defense, Donald Rumsfeld, carte blanche to transform the US armed forces and take full advantage of new technological capacities. This authority fed into the *Quadrennial Defense Review* (QDR2001)—released on 30 September 2001.[13] Although released shortly after the 11 September 2001 terrorist attacks, and presented as a document that absorbed the lessons of that dreadful event, QDR2001 was arguably the only strategy document crafted by the Bush Administration in a pre-11 September 2001 mindset. And a strong case could be made that, in addition to projecting what the new technologies, operational concepts and organisational structures would mean for force structure and military strategies, QDR2001 also reflected the philosophy that underpinned the 'grand strategy' developed in the Pentagon in 1992–93.

The QDR2001 essentially declared that the United States would seek to shape the security environment more directly and across a broader front than it had aspired to do in the past. A key judgement shaping the report was that the security outlook was so fluid that it would be dangerous for the United States to focus on who or where threats to its interests might arise. Instead, it would focus on how capabilities to harm US interests could develop over time and prepare to deal with such challenges wherever they might appear.

The report also made clear that the focus of US attention in strategic and security terms had shifted emphatically to Asia. This region is described as the most susceptible to military competition, containing a volatile mix of rising and declining powers, and as the possible source of a real military competitor to the United States. To reinforce this new strategic focus, and to distinguish it from the historical preoccupation with the Korean Peninsula, the QDR introduced a new region—the East Asian Littoral, defined as the region stretching from south of Japan through Australia and into the Bay of Bengal.

A further key judgement was to require that the capabilities of US forces deployed or stationed abroad be transformed so that they became lighter, more responsive and easier to sustain logistically, but also more lethal. The QDR2001 conveyed the impression of a Pentagon that now looked out upon the entire world as a battlespace and aspired to forces that could be surged quickly within or between regions to create, along with long-range precision strike forces, decisive and persistent military effects at any location. For the Asian theatre, with its vast distances and with the US forward presence heavily concentrated in North Asia, this requirement was also seen to put a premium on developing a wider network of austere bases and support facilities. At the same time, to avoid undue dependence on such bases and support facilities, QDR2001 called for the capability to conduct sustained operations at great distances with minimal support from within the theatre.

The fallout from the 11 September 2001 terrorist attacks on the United States meant that Washington's intent to give priority to Asia (the first time in at least 30 years that Asia had displaced Europe and the Middle East) never materialised. One consequence of this, it would seem, was that it strengthened the hand of those in Chinese policy circles who argued that the window of opportunity to give maximum priority to economic development, and gathering the political influence that flowed from success on this front without having to consider focused American counter-strategems, had been extended.

Despite the almost complete diversion of US political and military energies into Iraq since 2002, the *Quadrennial Defense Review* released in 2006 (QDR2006) basically developed and fine-tuned its predecessor.[14] The Pentagon remains committed to shifting away from large garrisons at fixed bases toward expeditionary forces operating out of austere forward bases. QDR2006 speaks undramatically of the need to conduct multiple, overlapping wars[15] —an indicator of how far the Pentagon has moved intellectually from the 2MRC era. Another QDR2001 theme, the need to tailor deterrent and defence strategies to a trilogy of distinctive threats—rogue powers, terrorist networks and near-peer competitors—is reiterated. The Iraq experience produced an important concession in that QDR2006 notes[16] that military force alone cannot succeed against dispersed non-state networks and that the real key lies in creating a global environment inhospitable to terrorism.[17]

QDR2006 also revived the question of China, and directly so rather than elliptically as in QDR2001. Despite China's strenuous claims to military weakness and technological backwardness, QDR2006 considered that 'China has the greatest potential to compete militarily with the United States and field disruptive military technologies that could over time offset traditional U.S. military advantages absent U.S. counter strategies'.[18] The report goes on to itemise the capabilities that China is giving priority to before observing that 'these capabilities, the vast distances of the Asian theater, China's continental depth, and the challenge of en route and in-theater U.S. basing place a premium on forces capable of sustained operations at great distances into denied areas'.[19] The US Navy objective is to place 50 per cent of its aircraft carriers (six ships) and 60 per cent of its submarines (over 30 boats) in the Pacific to support engagement, presence, and deterrence.[20]

The Pentagon's high tempo of operations, the emphasis on expeditionary forces surging to achieve synergistic effects and the blurring of regional boundaries has seen the end of the consolidated statement on the rewards of forward-deployment such as that quoted above from 1998. All the functions and objectives remain, but there is now a stronger disposition to blend these purposes into more operationalised characterisations of US military missions: irregular challenges (defeating terrorist networks); catastrophic challenges (preventing rogue regimes from acquiring or using WMD); and disruptive challenges (shaping the choices of states at strategic crossroads).

Taking stock

With Europe as the reference point, and setting aside the forces injected to prosecute the wars in Korea and Vietnam, the fixed elements of the US security posture in Asia have always appeared relatively thin—a limited spider web of bilateral 'spokes' radiating out from Washington. Still, it is likely that most political and foreign/security policy elites in the region would judge that this posture has been adequate to the task; that it has provided a sufficiency of confidence in the integrity of a basic regional order to underpin the region's impressive economic development.

It might also be agreed that the US posture has not been about micro-management of the region's affairs but instead directed at the big picture—the deterrence of the use or threat of use of force to secure fundamental change in the region's political and security order. Finally, it would probably be agreed that, with significant variations over the years in terms of intensity and directness, China has always ranked among the important targets whose thinking and actions the United States has endeavoured to influence. Since the demise of the Soviet Union, China has unquestionably been *the* most important target.

The long cycles in China-US relations over the past 50 years have been elegantly explored by James Mann in *About Face: A History of America's Curious Relationship with China, from Nixon to Clinton*.[21] China has never been enamoured of the US alliances with Asian states and the forward-deployed forces that attended these arrangements. But China's tolerance of these arrangements fluctuated pragmatically in response to factors like the state of China-Soviet relations, and whether the alliances continued to deliver outcomes of value to China, particularly effective constraints on Japanese military power but also a reliable stalemate on the Korean Peninsula. A more subtle consideration is that confidence in the US-backed security framework has permitted the smaller states in East Asia, especially those in Southeast Asia, to engage China unreservedly as a rewarding economic partner—a posture that has proved to be extremely beneficial for China.

There is speculation however that, from about the time of the near-confrontation with the United States over Taiwan in 1996, China's assessment has been that the direct and prominent US role in the security equation in East Asia was no longer in China's interests. Some point to China's relentless marketing of its new security concept, and the associated strong criticism of existing arrangements as hegemonic, anachronistic and reflective of a 'Cold War mentality', as evidence of this. Others suggest that while China may now be of this view, its political judgement remains that China must be patient and endure the status quo on the security front so that it can continue to give first priority to rebuilding its economic capacity.

Assuming that some such re-evaluation has occurred, the issue of interest becomes the main points of divergence in Chinese and American security interests and why these might now outweigh the benefits that once flowed from the US security presence and, to some extent, presumably continue to do so.

Taiwan is undoubtedly the most prominent and consequential of these points of divergence. This issue has bedevilled the China-US relationship since 1950 and has been at the heart of several major confrontations, including a couple of incidents in the 1950s that involved serious consideration by the United States of its nuclear options. China has made it clear that it would have no choice but to use force if Taiwan, as a perceived integral part of China, attempted to achieve formal independence. The United States is equally locked into the position that it cannot allow the status quo to be altered by force. There has been adequate 'wriggle room' between these positions to allow the issue to be continually finessed. Neither the United States nor China wants a war over Taiwan, and China has all but acknowledged that it would probably lose a military contest if the issue blew up in the medium-term future and the United States elected to get involved quickly and unreservedly. This prospect may have motivated the occasional warning from senior Chinese figures that China would not exclude escalation to the level of strategic nuclear threats against the United States.

In recent years, the concern has become that Beijing views a Taiwanese push for independence as an irreducible risk that necessitates, within the overall priority attached to 'peaceful development', the acquisition of military capabilities that will more reliably deter Taiwan even if it assumes US involvement. This has been the Pentagon's judgement for some time. QDR2006 reaffirmed this judgement, asserting that 'Chinese military modernization has accelerated since the mid-to-late 1990s in response to central leadership demands to develop military options against Taiwan scenarios'.[22]

The second specific issue arising from US military engagement in East Asia and involving a significant clash of important Chinese and US interests probably concerns Japan. Specifically, it would appear that the US-Japan alliance, once viewed by China as a constraint on Japan's acquisition of comprehensive conventional military capabilities and the 'normalisation' of Japanese attitudes toward the use of its armed forces to protect and advance the national interest, is now seen as a springboard for these developments. When the former was the case, it constituted a major consideration in China's reluctance to oppose the US alliance system. But while it is a weighty issue, it is diffuse in the sense that, unlike Taiwan, it does not contain a clear potential trigger for conflict with the United States. China-Japan territorial disputes, particularly with regards to the Diaoyutai Islands, clearly have the potential to involve Japan's alliance partner, but it still lacks the gravity of the Taiwan issue.

We should bear in mind, of course, that we do not require more than one clash of vital interests to produce a worst-case outcome for the security outlook in East Asia. Still, in examining how the prevailing US security posture toward East Asia might shape the China-US relationship in the future, it seems worthwhile to look beyond the specific and the concrete and to consider some of the more subjective or intangible dimensions of this issue. The United States has, over the post-war period, become comfortable and familiar with pre-eminence, not least in East Asia. Even under the Clinton Administration, it was rather clear that the United States also became increasingly comfortable with unipolarity and the expanded opportunities for leadership and influence associated with it. This was true even though the United States was aware that unipolarity also expanded its already formidable obligations and responsibilities and made the United States the target of choice for some gathering challenges that focused on irregular or asymmetric capabilities so as to bypass America's overwhelming conventional military power.

US rhetoric on the role it perceived itself playing arguably became more formulaic, more presumptive of its unique status as a natural state of affairs and, together with its support for (democratic) change in the nature of the regime in Beijing, was offensive to states like China that aspired to a greater role in shaping events, particularly in its immediate region. Many Chinese, it seems, anticipate and look forward to the progressive democratisation of governance in China, but this does not preclude resenting any suggestion that acceptance of a strong and influential China is in any way conditional on such a development. The inescapable corollary to US views on the role it is playing in East Asia is that there is no local player with the resources and the national qualities to perform this role as reliably as the United States—again an implicit message that China probably finds vaguely offensive.

This is not the first time that the United States has been accused of slipping onto 'auto-pilot' with respect to its engagement with East Asia. In the early 1990s, Winston Lord, then US Assistant Secretary of State for East Asian and Pacific Affairs in the Clinton Administration's first term, said in an internal memo (that was subsequently leaked) that the United States was seen in the region as something of a 'nanny' and that this was diminishing its standing and influence.

In addition, events like the Kosovo campaign in 1999, conducted with NATO over the objections (in the United Nations Security Council (UNSC)) of China and Russia, the 1995–96 clash over Taiwan, and awareness of the grand strategy articulated by the Pentagon in 1992–93, would have made China (and a number of other states) more uncertain that the United States would remain a 'benign hegemon'—a state that was ominously powerful without being an ominous power.

Under the Bush Administration, of course, this relatively subtle, to some extent unconscious and incremental, evolution in America's appreciation of the potential of its 'unipolar moment' was cast aside in favour of overt exploitation and determined defence of this status. Equally, this (neo-conservative) posture of deliberate dominance and of the forceful and proactive promotion of US interests and values (especially liberal democracy) has been thoroughly discredited.

That said, the United States will not soon, or readily, relinquish its position in East Asia. It has expended a great deal of treasure and not a little blood to establish and consolidate this position. Moreover, the impulses of power and prestige, not to mention the economic rewards from a region that is stable, progressively more democratic, and economically dynamic (including an increasingly open trading regime), will endure. The United States not only has the power to project itself into East Asia if it must; many if not most states in the region can be expected to continue to welcome a prominent US role into the indefinite future.

There are unmistakable signs that the United States is casting about for a less taxing mode of leadership and that it will exhibit greater acceptance of the inevitable but gradual erosion of its status as the unipolar power. Coral Bell of the Strategic and Defence Studies Centre (SDSC) has speculated that the prevailing and emerging circumstances may be relatively conducive to global governance by a *concert of powers* rather than the *balance of powers*, implicit in the expectation that the global system will trend back to multipolarity.[23] A concert of powers, clearly, is a more collegiate arrangement and more accommodating of significant power differentials among participating states.

The most conspicuous sign from Washington was the speech in September 2005 by the then US Deputy Secretary of State, Robert B. Zoellick, advocating that China think in terms of being a 'responsible stakeholder' in the international system, to accept responsibility to strengthen the system that has contributed so much to its success, and to look to working with the United States to 'shape the future international system'.[24] Other signs include a preparedness to engage North Korea and Iran on their nuclear ambitions rather than simply demand that they change their ways.

The United States and China cannot escape a long process of adjustment to the gradual transformation in their relative strategic weight. The twilight of the unipolar era will be measured in decades. A great deal of statesmanship and diplomacy will be called for to prevent the inevitable frictions that will attend this process from degenerating and hardening into deeper animosities. If this is a broadly reasonable prognosis, the earlier these two countries commit to a process of determined engagement and to building robust channels of communication and dialogue, the greater the likelihood of success over the longer term. To the extent that we have a real choice as to whether unipolarity fades gradually into a multipolar balance of power or a concert, that choice rests primarily with the United States. Yet there is much that the other major powers can do to shape US thinking.

At various times over the past 30 years or so, the United States has assigned carriage of the US-China relationship to very senior people: Zbigniew Brzezinski and Alexander Haig come to mind, although I have no knowledge of who their Chinese counterparts may have been. What is striking, however, is that there has been nothing comparable to the intellectual engagement that Henry Kissinger and Zhou Enlai managed to build during 1971–75. The danger, perhaps, is that both countries will remain reluctant for some time to give such 'determined engagement' a real chance. In Washington, which often finds it difficult to think long-term, China may continue to be viewed as too distant an issue to be placed at the top of the agenda. Beijing, equally, may view any fundamental engagement with the United States in the near term as too risky, because it will be seen as engaging on the modalities of a US-designed world with a United States that is still comprehensively more powerful than China.

ENDNOTES

[1] See Robert Kagan, 'A retreat From Power?', *Commentary*, July 1995, pp. 19–25.

[2] Quoted in Patrick E. Tyler, 'US Strategy Plan Calls for Ensuring No Rivals Develop: A One Superpower World', *New York Times*, 8 March 1992.

[3] President George H.W. Bush, *National Security Strategy of the United States*, White House, Washington, DC, August 1991. [emphasis added]

[4] James Mann, *Rise of the Vulcans: The History of Bush's War Cabinet*, Penguin, New York, 2004, p. 211.

[5] Secretary of Defense Dick Cheney, *Defense Strategy for the 1990s: The Regional Defense Strategy*, Washington, DC, January 1993.

[6] Cheney, *Defense Strategy for the 1990s: The Regional Defense Strategy*, p. 2.

[7] Cheney, *Defense Strategy for the 1990s: The Regional Defense Strategy*, p. 4.

[8] Cheney, *Defense Strategy for the 1990s: The Regional Defense Strategy*, p. 4.

[9] Cheney, *Defense Strategy for the 1990s: The Regional Defense Strategy*, p. 8.

[10] President George W. Bush, Graduation Speech at the United States Military Academy, West Point, New York, 1 June 2002.

[11] Secretary of Defense William Cohen, *The United States Security Strategy for the East Asia-Pacific Region*, Department of Defense, November 1998, p. 16, available at <http://www.dod.mil/pubs/easr98/easr98.pdf>, accessed 17 June 2009.

[12] Cohen, *The United States Security Strategy for the East Asia-Pacific Region*, pp. 9–10.

[13] Department of Defense, *Quadrennial Defense Review Report*, 30 September 2001.

[14] Department of Defense, *Quadrennial Defense Review Report* (QDR2006), 6 February 2006, available at <http://www.comw.org/qdr/qdr2006.pdf>, accessed 17 June 2009.

[15] Department of Defense, QDR2006, p. 4.

[16] Department of Defense, QDR2006, p. 9.

[17] Department of Defense, QDR2006, p. 22.
[18] Department of Defense, QDR2006, p. 29.
[19] Department of Defense, QDR2006, p. 30.
[20] Department of Defense, QDR2006, p. 47.
[21] James Mann, *About Face: A History of America's Curious Relationship with China, from Nixon to Clinton*, Alfred A. Knopf, New York, 1999.
[22] Department of Defense, QDR2006, p. 29.
[23] Coral Bell, 'The Twilight of the Unipolar World', *The National Interest*, Winter 2005, pp. 1–12.
[24] Robert B. Zoellick, *Whither China: From Membership to Responsibility*, US Department of State, 21 September 2005 (remarks to the National Committee on US-China Relations, New York).

Chapter 8

The Role of the United States in the Future Security Architecture for East Asia—from the Perspective of China-US Military-to-Military Interaction

Lu Dehong

> What remains unchanged transcending all changes is benevolence. Knowing only what is changing without knowing what remains unchanged, the humankind will never enjoy peace.
>
> —Xong Shili (1884–1968), Chinese philosopher

The East Asian region is in a grand transitional period. Its economic importance to world prosperity and its potential contribution to global peace are increasing. Nevertheless, the region, especially Northeast Asia, is not only the most militarised region in the world, but is also a region to date lacking any single regional organisation through which conflicts can be handled.[1] Economic cooperation and military hedging between major powers enhances simultaneously. The deviation of economy and security is not in the interest of lasting peace and prosperity and the fundamental interests of all concerned countries.

Whether it is in accord with the expectation of East Asian countries and their internal political groups or not, the United States will be the cornerstone of any meaningful and feasible future security architecture for East Asia. What is not certain is whether the United States will fulfil this role in a hegemonic security architecture or a harmonious one. There are sets of factors, internal and external to the United States, together with interactions between the major powers, which will shape the role of the United States in the future security architecture of East Asia. The direction, pace and structure of such an architecture will depend on the synergistic effects of these factors and interactions.

China is the strategic focus of the US East Asia security policy. In a major bi-partisan effort to devise a new national security strategy in 2005, the final report of a Princeton University study pointed out that the rise of China is one of the most important events in the early twenty-first century, and viewed China as one example of a major threat and challenge.[2] The US security community is watchful of China's military development. The Pentagon's annual report on the topic is but the tip of the iceberg. China-US military relations are pivotal for East Asian security. They will determine the outlook and nature of the future security architecture in the region. Unfortunately, because of asymmetric US information and influence, the term and logic for an East Asian security architecture has been largely defined in an American way, shaping international perceptions on Chinese military issues and on the China-US military-to-military relationship.[3] It is in the interest of all concerned parties and of future generations in the Asia-Pacific region to understand the root dynamics of this relationship and its impact on any future regional security architecture.

Internal factors: The sources of US conduct

As the extension of the US national will, interest, power and strategy, its security policy and posture toward East Asia and China is inevitably influenced directly or indirectly by the same internal factors that shape its overall power and policy. To make sense of the US role in East Asia security, we have to consider these internal factors. Graham Allison's framework of rational actor model, organisational behaviour model, and governmental politics model is an elegant conceptual guide for an explanation and prediction of US foreign policy.[4] In addition to Graham Allison's models, the author would argue that a military–economy synergy model should be considered for a comprehensive understanding on the root cause of US behaviour.

Rational actor model

The starting point for all rational actors is their political objective. Since the end of the Cold War, the US strategic community has been seeking a new grand design or architecture to guide the planning of future forces; that is, a successor to 'containment' of the Soviet Union. In essence, this process seeks to reconfirm US strategic objectives. The distinctive character of current US strategic objectives can be summarised as the following three points.

The first aspect is freedom of action. In former US President George W. Bush's words, 'the U.S. needs no permission slip from the United Nations or anybody else to act'.[5] This view of its options, including military objectives, is the most important difference between the United States and almost all other countries. Freedom of action is the organising thread of the US national security, defence, and military strategy, as well as its national space policy. Freedom of action in reality is the capability to create events, make rules—'the authority to set the global agenda'.[6]

The second aspect is peerless military advantages. Freedom of action is impossible without 'military supremacy'. 'At their core, both liberty and law must be backed up by force.'[7] The United States takes military supremacy as the core pillar of its world status, and wants to keep it permanently. Thus, redefining war on American terms (as Bush described it in February 2001),[8] to dissuade any military competitor from developing disruptive or other capabilities, has become the objective itself.

The final aspect is to prevent any other country from dominating Eurasia. This point will be discussed later in the chapter.

To help define these objectives, the worst-case scenario is widely used, indeed over used, in US strategic planning. As the classical military planning method, worst-case scenario is not without merit. However, if the history of the Cold War told us anything, it should be that the so-called realistic mindset plus worst-case scenario led to an unnecessary and dangerous arms race between the United States and the former Soviet Union. The benefit of worst-case scenario cannot make up for its inherent cost and risk. Closer observation suggests that worst-case scenario and threat exaggeration is a means to mobilise internal resources rather than a rational assessment of the external environment. As the leading military power today, if the United States can find reasons to use a worst-case scenario, other countries have far more reason to do so. In fact, in the author's opinion, since the end of the Second World War, the United States has taken the lead in both the use of worst-case scenario, and in creating security dilemmas.

Governmental politics model and organisational behaviour model

David R. Obey, former chairman of the US Congress House Appropriations Committee, has said that the way Congress reviews the Pentagon 'has certainly become dysfunctional. Congress, instead of being the watchdog, is the dog that has to be watched. ... The Congress committees entrusted to oversee the Pentagon budgets act like "a pork machine"'. He termed it 'outrageous' for the US Air Force to assert that

> the reason we have to build the F-22 in the first place is because we sold so many F-16s around the world that we have to keep a qualitative edge over them. So when we say we will put a limit on your ability to sell the F-16s abroad, they say, You can't do that because it costs jobs.[9]

Obey's words illustrate the impact of US Congress 'pork-barrel politics' on military policy. Internal political consideration, military service parochialism, and interest-seeking defence industries combine to form a Political–Military–Industrial Complex, which plays 'the art of the possible' in respect of the defence budget. Former US Defense Secretary James Schlesinger said that it was not easy to 'keep the DOD a relatively harmonious whole'. He went on to say that 'many possible decisions, which would seem logically sound, will nonetheless be avoided, simply for the purpose of maintaining peace within the family. ... The net result is the creation of side payments for almost everybody'.[10] RAND Corporation-based expert Kevin N. Lewis pointed out that

> as a result of political influences, externally generated demands, and organizational inertia, even if we had an agreed long-range defense program, the odds of seeing it through to fruition would be poor. This effect, which I called discipline gap in planning, can have serious consequences.[11]

These 'serious consequences' were and are not merely within the United States. In fact, US scholar Gordon R. Mitchell believes that the Cold War arms race came from an internal American arms race: 'The Soviet Union was less an instigator of the arms race and more the straggling follower of a massive unilateral American military buildup.'[12]

The net results of 'rational actor, governmental politics and organisational behaviour' are grave and dangerous, which include but are not limited to the habit of threat exaggeration and huge defence expenditure. The United States had 'a tendency throughout the Cold War to exaggerate the threat'; and this tendency persists into the post Cold War era. On the myth of the 'missile gap' in the early 1960s, one US scholar has observed that 'Soviet force levels were a factor in the Pentagon's calculations, but were not the most important by any manner of means. In other words, U.S. deployment followed its own logic, and that implied a prior strategy'.[13] Meanwhile, Robert H. Johnson has said that 'the interaction between psychology, politics, and changes in the international environment are the keys to the explanation of U.S. conceptions of the threat and of the tendency of those conceptions to overstate the threat'.[14] As Columbia University history professor Carol Gluck pointed out, 'without some way to transcend our differences we are doomed to reenact the hostilities toward others that seem to lodge so deeply in our political unconscious'. The Working Group on Relative Threat Assessment of the Princeton Project on National Security noted that, 'in practice, bureaucratic and commercial incentives have a strong influence on the threats that are considered and treated seriously by the U.S.'[15] The habit and skills of threat exaggeration, internal political process, and armed services' inertia, have serious implications for the future security architecture for East Asia.

Military–Economy synergy model

How to explain the uniqueness of US strategic objectives? In almost all other countries, military policy and defence experts take the following three points as basic presumptions: the aim of the military is to defend; the military is the tool of foreign policy; and military expenditure is a burden to economy. Even though many US experts share this perspective, US national policy can be described as its obverse: the aim of the military is freedom of action; foreign policy can be the tool of the military; and military expenditure can be the catalyst for the economy and an important source of core economic competence for the next generation. Richard R. Nelson, a US expert on national innovation, points out that defence expenditure is one of the two most important factors in understanding the US national innovation system.[16]

According to US scholar Diane Kunz, 'the US built its Cold War hegemony on the base created by the World War II production miracle. Washington then converted the bipolar geopolitical confrontation into fuel that powered its domestic economy. This synergy proved crucial'.[17] A RAND Corporation report echoes Kunz's observation by saying that

> national power is ultimately a product of the interaction of two components: a country's ability to dominate the cycles of economic innovation at a given point in time and, thereafter, to utilize the fruits of this domination to produce effective military capabilities that, in turn, reinforce existing economic advantages while producing a stable political order.[18]

The military–economy synergy manifests itself as a chain of cause and effect relations:

> Whoever controls space, therefore, will control the world's oceans. Whoever controls the oceans will control the patterns of global commerce. Whoever controls the patterns of global commerce will be the wealthiest power in the world. Whoever is the wealthiest power in the world will be able to control space.[19]

Put another way, it is a military–market nexus:

> (1) Look for resources and ye shall find, but … (2) no stability, no market; (3) no growth, no stability; (4) no resources, no growth; (5) no infrastructure, no resources; (6) no money, no infrastructure; (7) no rules, no money; (8) no security, no rules; (9) no Leviathan, no security; (10) no (American) will, no Leviathan. Understanding the military–market link is not just good business, it is good national security strategy.[20]

All empires enjoyed strong linkages between their military and the other sources of national power. The link could be military–land, military–commerce, military–industry, or military–finance. The United States is no exception. The only difference in its case is that it has compresses all these links into some 230 years rather than thousands of years. Kunz accurately points out that, in 1946, George Kennan explained in his 'long telegram' that, for domestic reasons, 'the Soviet Union needed a permanent enemy':

Soviet leaders are driven by necessities of their own past and present position to put forth a dogma which depicts the outside world as evil, hostile and menacing. ... [Kennan] was right—not only about the Soviet Union but about the United States as well.[21]

External Factors

China

Since the mid-1990s, US military strategic focus has shifted to East Asia, with China being one of the main driving factors, if not the only one in the longer-term.[22] The recent Iraq conflict and the global 'war on terror' have disrupted the process to some extent, but have not changed its direction. China is still the country at the 'strategic crossroads', needing to be hedged.[23] It is not a surprise to learn that, 'China is in the central place in U.S. strategic planning' and that 'for more than a decade the main efforts of Pentagon force planning have been preparing to fight with the big one (China)'.[24] In view of the tension over the Taiwan Strait and the 'uncertainty of future China choices', China will be the most significant factor in US military strategy. The Pentagon takes a China-US military conflict as the standard scenario on which to focus its force planning, military and war gaming exercises, and its transformation related activities.[25]

How much is rational or irrational in the above American judgements and measures towards China is discussed below. At this point, it is helpful to know the US side of the story. Thomas Barnett pointed out that the

China threat has a close relation with the interest of the U.S. military services. After the disappearance of the Soviet threat, the U.S. military services do not want to lose their status in American national security. They use the China threat as a convenient justification for budget requirements.[26]

US arms sales to Taiwan, which have a fatal influence on China-US military-to-military relations, can also be explained partly by the US internal political behaviour model.[27]

US alliances

Military alliances are the pillars of America's military posture in East Asia. The adjustment and enhancement of bilateral military alliances, as well as building networks of alliances and various security partners, constitute the core of US security policy toward this region. Nonetheless, Aaron Friedberg, then deputy national security adviser of former US Vice President Dick Cheney, pointed out that alliances are not, or should not be, ends in themselves; they are means for the attainment of larger strategic objectives. The collapse of the Soviet Union leaves China as the only country that could conceivably be capable, over the next several decades, of establishing itself as the preponderant power in Asia. It follows that the fundamental aim of American strategy in Asia must be not merely to promote stability, but rather to prevent Chinese hegemony.[28]

In fact, to prevent any other country from dominating Eurasia is a lasting US strategic objective. It is the precondition for America's ability to preserve its global dominance and freedom of action. This view of the United States as the 'supreme power' was outlined in the draft *Defense Planning Guidance*, drawn up in 1992 under the supervision of the then US Undersecretary for Defense Policy Paul Wolfowitz:

> Our first objective is to prevent the reemergence of a new rival. This is the dominant consideration underlying the new regional defense strategy and requires that we endeavor to prevent any hostile power from dominating a region whose resources would, under consolidated control, be sufficient to generate global power. There are three additional aspects to this objective. First, the U.S. must show the leadership necessary to establish and protect a new order that holds the promise of convincing potential competitors that they need not aspire to a greater role or pursue an aggressive posture to protect their legitimate interests. Second, in the non-defense areas, we must account sufficiently for the interests of the advanced industrial nations to discourage them from challenging our leadership or seeking to overturn the established political and economic order. Finally, we must maintain the mechanisms for deterring competitors from even aspiring to a larger regional or global role.[29]

For this strategic objective, it is necessary for the United States to sustain measured tension within Eurasia. Without tension, the US military presence and the quality of military alliances will be difficult to maintain. French scholar Tod Foley pointed out that 'Europeans do not understand why the US refuses to resolve the Israel-Palestinian issue, although it can make a difference. They even wonder if the Americans want to keep this issue as a permanent hot point'. According to Foley, 'America is willing to create an atmosphere of tension, some kind of limited but dangerous war state'.[30] The fundamental principle of US grand strategy over the past century has been to manipulate the Eurasian balance of power to prevent the emergence of any hegemonic powers that are capable of harnessing Eurasia's vast resources and challenging US naval supremacy. The implementation of this strategy turned on the twin principles of economy of force and indirect action. Economy of force was realised by using allies to bear the strategic burden and the brunt of combat. Indirect action involved never attacking an enemy frontally. Weakening an opponent through internal or external opposition, and relying on economic power to produce the pre-conditions of victory, was preferred to any premature test of military strength.[31]

As to multilateral security mechanisms, the United States assigns them to a supplement role. Former US President Bill Clinton put forward that 'the ARF [ASEAN Regional Forum] and other multilateral security initiatives are a way to supplement our alliances and forward military presence, not supplant them'.[32] It seems quite logical that the Bush Administration should do its best to marginalise the role of the United Nations—the most important global multilateral security mechanism.

China-US military-to-military interactions

China-US military-to-military relations are the weakest link in the overall bilateral relationship. We know from past experience that whenever disturbance or crisis has occurred in China-US relations, military-to-military relations have suffered first; and that these have been the last to be restored—well after the resumption of bilateral relations. This pattern is not in the interests of China, the United States, or the Asia-Pacific region.

At present, both countries have the intention to improve bilateral military relations. Nonetheless, before any durable progress can be made, we need to think more deeply about the essence of the problem. From the discussion above, we know that China is at the heart of US strategic thinking about East Asia. In the near-term, the US military has detailed operational plans to fight China during the course of any crisis in the Taiwan Strait. In the longer-term, the US military is taking various measures to hedge future uncertainties regarding China. Worse still, the near-term and longer-term considerations are mutually enforcing, which could potentially lead China-US military-to-military interactions into a kind of vicious spiral. Against this background, the best both countries could achieve together would be to prevent the worst outcomes, rather than to think what they could do together for better regional and global security.

US military policy toward Taiwan serves as a master-switch that decisively influences the direction, quality and process of China-US military interaction. China-US military relations are in inverse proportion to US-Taiwan military relations—the closer the US-Taiwan ties; the farther away the China-US military relationship. Against such a background, minor problems in China-US military relations raise significant issues which, in turn, can become big problems. And big problems can become insurmountable ones. Issues of transparency, code of conduct and reciprocity will continue to block the way if both sides fail to establish stronger mutual trust about their strategic goals. Everyone knows that preventing Taiwan from making reckless moves is the strategic bottom line for

China—a line that has to be defended at any price, against any enemy. The Chinese military has to prepare itself for this most difficult and complex situation. This is the overwhelming mission for the Chinese military. It is therefore unrealistic to expect a substantive increase of transparency about China's core military capabilities.

Some Americans think that China will handle its relations with other Asian countries and the United States in the way China treats Taiwan. This is wrong. There is a fundamental difference between the two. The nature of the Taiwan issue is domestic and the rest are external. Thus, US-Taiwan military relations should maintain a respectful distance from China's bottom line. Richard Haass is right in noting that 'the governments of the world's principal powers will cooperate with the U.S. only if there is a context in which their fundamental national interests are seen by their own publics to be protected'.[33]

As to America's longer-term concerns, we know uncertainties exist since the present generation cannot and should not make decisions for future generations. However, how should we prepare ourselves for such future uncertainties and what are we going to leave to succeeding generations? Are we leaving them operational concepts and weapons platforms to fight wars or the habits and a tradition of mutual trust and cooperation? Questions like this should be discussed among all the parties. Unfortunately, the Taiwan issue is continually blocking the way.

Former US Secretary of Defense William Perry and Assistant Secretary of Defense Ashton Carter have observed that China cannot be expected to fight with bows and arrows.[34] In other words, China's military capabilities will certainly develop along with its growing economy. Should Chinese military development follow certain rules? What strategic understanding should be reached with Asia-Pacific countries in general and the United States in particular? What are rules of the road to maintain regional and global security? What constitutes the legitimate use of force? We can and should discuss these issues. After all, China does not have any intention to challenge other countries, especially the United States, militarily. However, external factors relating to Taiwan have stopped us from engaging in substantial discussion. The conclusion is that the Taiwan question effectively pollutes the possibility of developing a meaningful and workable security architecture for East Asia.

The defensive nature of China's defence policy

There are many articles and books discussing, guessing or interpreting China's 'grand strategy'; and it is quite strange that the majority of these works do not pay attention to or even mention the simple facts. In my analysis, the six commonsense facts about China defence policy are as follows.

First, China takes it as national policy to oppose military alliances. It is commonsense that any country, even one as powerful militarily as the United States, that might want to launch strategic offensive operations towards another country, must have military alliances. This national policy of China points clearly to the fact that China has no intention of launching strategic offensive operations against other countries. When China says it is a 'peace-loving country', it is definitely not empty rhetoric.

Second, China takes it as national policy to keep the central role of the United Nations in maintaining international peace and security. This means that it is impossible for China to behave unilaterally on international security issues.

Third, China remains firmly committed to the policy of no first use of nuclear weapons, no use of nuclear weapons against non-nuclear weapon states or nuclear-weapon-free zones, and stands for the comprehensive prohibition and complete elimination of nuclear weapons. China is the only nuclear weapon state that has such a policy.

Fourth, China has called for an international pact to prohibit the weaponisation of outer space. If the United States cares about the 'future uncertainties' of China's military development, it can address these in the domain of outer space by joining China in negotiating such a pact. The US national space policy makes it clear that it fully understands, perhaps better than any other country, how important outer space is for future military operations.

Fifth, China honours its commitment to international arms control and non-proliferation.[35]

Sixth, on the principles of the use of force, China is fully committed to the UN Charter, which means that, beyond matters of self-defence, China will not use force internationally unless authorised by the United Nations Security Council (UNSC). Regarding self-defence, China will not use force unless facing utmost provocation, when it is the last resort, and when an opposing country fires the first shot.

Does China have 'a grand strategy'? The answer is definitely 'no', if one has a true understanding of China's culture. What do the Chinese people want? For thousands of years, what they have wanted is encapsulated in the saying 'Good weather for the crops, the country prospers and the people are at peace' (*Feng Tiao yu shun, Guo Tai Min An*).[36] No more, no less. This has been the dream of the Chinese historically. It is the dream of today's Chinese, and it will be the dream of future Chinese. The Chinese are defined by China's culture. The key to the continuation of Chinese civilisation is exactly this culture. The Chinese do not aspire to be number one, but they do long for a harmonious domestic and international society. This was well understood by Arnold Toynbee.[37] To explain and predict China's 'strategy' and future behaviour in US terms and in the logic of so-called 'realism' is almost meaningless.

Conclusion: to start from commonsense

Chinese philosopher Xong Shili (1884–1968) said that 'what remains unchanged transcending all changes is benevolence. Knowing only what is changing without knowing what remains unchanged, the humankind will never enjoy peace'.[38] Albert Einstein said that 'everything has changed except our manner of thinking'. Both Xong Shili and Einstein are right. This has been, is and will be one of the most important tenets of commonsense. The best way, and perhaps the only viable way, to discuss the future security architecture for East Asia is to start from commonsense.

A new world of closer and closer global interdependence is coming. With increasing interdependence, the common interests of major countries are enlarging and deepening. This is the objective and the true reality. The sources of difference or conflict are either subordinate or subjective, and in most cases they are merely distorted perceptions or opinions. In order to bridge the gap between distorted perceptions and true reality, we need new definitions and concepts regarding power and international relationships. If factors such as global warming, and the outbreaks of Severe Acute Respiratory Syndrome (SARS) and the H5N1 and H1N1 influenzas tell us something or anything, it is that as long as we breathe the same air, we have to share the same destiny. Nothing is more important than this common destiny. The potential supply of global and regional security exceeds our collective security requirements, thanks to the asymmetry between the military expenditure of the only superpowers and of major powers, and humanitarian assistance. The gap between global security requirements and the capacity to supply this security is a matter of will rather than of capacity—a matter of how to use force rather than of no use of force. Nonetheless, the gap between supply and requirement is growing. People in Africa, who have suffered so much for so long, are still suffering. Africans are forgotten, even though the continent's resources are not. Against this backdrop, pretending to be 'tough' to other major powers under the guise of so called 'realism' is itself unreal, and so short-sighted. Realism is an anachronism in a global era.

William Fulbright, former Chairman of the US Congress foreign relations committee, said that we should see the world as others see it:

> Today we need a leadership that recognizes that the fundamental challenge in this nuclear hi-tech era is one of psychology and education in the field of human relations. It is not the kind of problem that is likely to be resolved by expertise—even the sophisticated expertise of our most gifted military thinkers, who delight in exotic weapons systems

and strategic doctrines that threaten the solvency of the richest nations as well as their physical survival. The attributes upon which we must draw are the human attributes of compassion and common sense, of intellect and creative imagination, and of empathy and understanding between cultures.[39]

It will be in everyone's interest to jointly explore a shared vision based on common interests. Mutual strategic confidence will flow from taking every opportunity to maximise the common interest. It will also be in everyone's interest to explore positive scenarios to balance the established worst-case scenario. We should and must be extremely cautious in applying the concepts of worst-case scenario and hedging in military planning. These strategic planning tools may be useful, but over-use of them may lead to unpalatable consequences. Judging from the lessons of the US-Soviet arms race, the United States and the Soviet Union needlessly wasted resources on a tremendous scale.

What is worse, the risks involved were much higher than the potential benefits that were realistically on offer. Only by guiding military policies on the base of common interests, and by exercising strong discipline to suppress the dominance of worse-case scenarios, will we be able to avoid strategic confrontation.

It is encouraging that some Americans have similar thinking. Ashton Carter and William Perry put forward the term 'responsible hedging'. They

> point out that since Chinese military leaders cannot predict the future, they will prepare for the worst even as they hope for the best. Hedging is contagious. During the Cold War, hedging and worst-case-scenario assumptions led to a dangerous and expensive arms race.[40]

The final report of the Princeton Project on National Security pointed out that any new national security strategy 'should be interest-based rather than threat-based, and grounded in hope rather than in fear'.[41] Richard Haass is right in saying that 'most global issues require global responses'. No single country, no matter how powerful, can contend successfully on its own with transnational challenges. An effective multilateralism is based on keeping a respectful distance from the core interest of other major powers:

> The goal of U.S. foreign policy should not simply be to maintain a world defined by U.S. military superiority. ... To have a chance of succeeding, the U.S. will need to view other major powers less as rivals and more as partners. The U.S. will have to accept some constraints on its freedom of action.

All of which brings us to the fundamental argument about opportunity:

The question is what Americans and others make of this moment. Time, resources, and potential have already been squandered. A different foreign policy, one based on promoting the world's integration while the opportunity to do so still exists, is urgently necessary.[42]

China's President, Hu Jintao, instructed China's military to regard making a major contribution to the maintenance of global peace and the promotion of common development as one of its historic missions. This is China's historic offer to the world and should not be refused. We Chinese are grateful to Australians when something bad happens to overseas Chinese in the South Pacific region; it has been Australia that has taken the lead and made a vital difference. We understand that China has its share of responsibility for regional and international affairs, and a duty to behave similarly. This is the commonsense approach for China-Australia security relations. We can see no reason why China and Australia cannot be closer security partners. If partnerships among all the major powers in Asia-Pacific region can be forged in this spirit, a future security architecture based on common interests and a shared vision will begin to take shape. In any case, what matters is what is remembered and emulated, not what is hated and resisted.[43] What matters is not to be more powerful or to be number one. What matters is what you do with your potential—create or destroy. What matters is to give rather than to take. Benevolence is humanity, which truly decides the greatness of any nation.

ENDNOTES

[1] Niklas Swanström, Mikael Weissman and Emma Björnehed, 'Introduction', in Niklas Swanström (ed.), *Conflict Prevention and Conflict Management in Northeast Asia*, Central Asia-Caucasus Institute and Silk Road Studies Program, John Hopkins University, Washington, DC, 2005, p. 9, available at <http://www.isdp.eu/node/1153>, accessed 17 June 2009.

[2] *Forging a world of Liberty Under Law: U.S. National Security Strategy for the 21st Century*, Final Report of Princeton Project on National Security, Princeton University, Princeton, 2006, available at <http://www.princeton.edu/~ppns/report/FinalReport.pdf>, accessed 17 June 2009.

[3] Some China scholars, deeply influenced by US international relations and strategy theories, talk and write in US terms and logic, even when sometimes criticising US security policy. The terms and logic include, but are far from limited to, 'realist', 'nationalism', 'soft power', ' China-US structural, strategic contradiction', and 'the relation of established superpower and superpower candidate'. It is the author's opinion that this kind of influence would distort rather than facilitate a healthy understanding of China-US relations and the true issues of Asian security.

[4] Graham Allison and Philip Zelikow, 'Introduction' in *Essence of Decision: Explaining the Cuban Missile Crisis*, 2nd edition, Longman, Reading, MA, 1999.

[5] Former US President George W. Bush's 2004 State of the Union Address, 20 January 2004, available at <http://whitehouse.georgewbush.org/news/2004/012004-SOTU.asp>, accessed 17 June 2009.

[6] Ron Huisken, *The Road to War on Iraq*, Canberra Papers on Strategy and Defence no.148, Strategic and Defence Studies Centre, The Australian National University, Canberra, 2003, p. 55.

[7] *Forging a world of Liberty Under Law: U.S. National Security Strategy for the 21st Century*, p. 8.

[8] George W. Bush, 'Remarks by the President to the troops and Personnel', Norfolk Naval Air Station, Norfolk, VA, 13 February 2001, available at <http://www.whitehouse.gov/news/releases/20010213-1.html>, accessed 5 May 2008.

[9] George C. Wilson, *This War Really Matters: Inside the Fight for Defense Dollars*, CQ Press, Washington, DC, 2000, pp. 115–17.

[10] Peter L. Hays (ed.), *American Defense Policy*, 7th edition, Johns Hopkins University Press, Baltimore, 1997, pp. 103 and 107.

[11] Paul K. Davis (ed.), *New Challenges for Defense Planning: Rethinking How Much Is Enough*, RAND Corporation, Santa Monica, 1994, p. 102, available at <http://www.rand.org/pubs/monograph_reports/MR400/>, accessed 17 June 2009.

[12] Gordon R. Mitchell, *Strategic Deception: Rhetoric, Science, and Politics in Missile Defense Advocacy*, Michigan State University Press, East Lansing, 2000, p. 31.

[13] Walter A. McDougall, *The Heavens and the Earth: A Political History of the Space Age*, John Hopkins University Press, Baltimore, 1997, p. 332.

[14] Robert H. Johnson, *Improbable Dangers: U.S. Conceptions of Threat in the Cold War and after*, St Martin's Press, New York, 1997, p. 2.

[15] *Forging a world of Liberty Under Law: U.S. National Security Strategy for the 21st Century*, p. 8.

[16] Richard R. Nelson, *National Innovation System: A Comparative Analysis*, Oxford University Press, New York, pp. 29–30.

[17] Diane B. Kunz, *Butter and Guns: America's Cold War Economic Diplomacy*, The Free Press, New York, 1997, p. 2.

[18] Ashley J. Tellis, Janice Bially, Christopher Layne, Melissa McPherson and Jerry M. Sollinger, *Measuring National Power in the Postindustrial Age: Analyst's Handbook*, RAND Corporation, Santa Monica, 2000, p. 4, available at <http://rand.org/pubs/monograph_reports/MR1110.1/>, accessed 17 June 2009.

[19] George Friedman and Meredith Friedman, *The Future of War: Power, Technology and American World Dominance in the Twenty-first Century*, Crown Publishers, New York, 1996, p. 411.

[20] Thomas P.M. Barnett, 'Glossary' in *Blueprint for Action: A Future Worth Creating*, G.P. Putnam & Sons, New York, 2005, p. xvii.

[21] Kunz, *Butter and Guns: America's Cold War Economic Diplomacy*, p. 328. Similar observations can be found in other materials. In 1999, Samuel Huntington noted: 'At a 1997 Harvard conference, scholars reported that the elites of countries comprising at least two-thirds of the world's people—Chinese, Russians, Indians, Arabs, Muslims, and Africans—see the United States as the single greatest threat to their societies. They do not regard the United States as a military threat, but as a menace to their integrity, autonomy, prosperity, and freedom of action. They view it as intrusive, interventionist, exploitative, unilateralist, hegemonic, hypocritical, and applying double standards, engaging in what they label 'financial imperialism' and 'intellectual colonialism', with a foreign policy driven overwhelmingly by domestic politics.' (Huntington quoted in Robert S. McNamara and James G. Blight, *Wilson's Ghost: Reducing the Risk of Conflict, Killing, and Catastrophe in the 21st Century*, Public Affairs, New York, 2001, p. 52)

[22] 'China has the potential to become a major military power in Asia'. The United States will keep 'the core capability to fight two major theatre wars in overlapping time frames', and ensure that the United States 'has sufficient military capabilities to defeat aggression by a larger adversary'. 'Of the major and emerging powers, China has the greatest potential to compete militarily with the United States'. See former US Secretary of Defense William S. Cohen, *Report of the Quadrennial Defense Review*, May 1997, available at <http://se2.isn.ch/serviceengine/FileContent?serviceID=ESDP&fileid=76C8F71A-89B7-5A1D-F9E9-B4851BF35DC0&lng=en>, accessed 17 June 2009; and former US Secretary of Defense, Donald Rumsfeld, *Quadrennial Defense Review Report*, US Department of Defense, 6 February 2006, available at <http://www.defenselink.mil/pubs/pdfs/QDR20060203.pdf >, accessed 17 June 2009.

[23] *National Security Strategy of the United States of America*, March 2006, available at <http://georgewbush-whitehouse.archives.gov/nsc/>, accessed 17 June 2009.

[24] Thomas P.M. Barnett, *The Pentagon's New Map: War and Peace in the Twenty-first Century*, Penguin Group, New York, 2004, p. 181.

[25] Jonathan Pollack, *Strategic Surprise? Sino-American relations in the 21st century*, US Navy War College Press, Newport, RI, 2003.

[26] Barnett, *The Pentagon's New Map: War and Peace in the Twenty-first Century*, p. 108.

[27] Zhang Qinming and Luo Binhui, 'Foreign Policy Decision-Making Models and Analysis on Determining Factors of American Arms Sale Policy', *American Studies Quarterly*, Institute of American Studies, Chinese Academy of Social Sciences, Beijing, March 2006.

28 Robert Kagan and William Kristol (eds), *Present Dangers: Crisis and Opportunity in American Foreign and Defense Policy*, Encounter Books, New York, 2000, pp. 198–99.

29 Draft Defense Planning Guidance quoted in Patrick E. Tyler, 'US Strategy Plan Calls for Insuring No Rivals Develop: A One-Superpower World', *New York Times*, 8 March 1992.

30 Translated by the author from the Chinese version. Tod Foley, *The Decline of the American Empire*, World Knowledge Press, Beijing, 2003, p. 7.

31 Friedman and Friedman, *The Future of War: Power, Technology and American World Dominance in the Twenty-first Century*, p. 97.

32 US Department of Defense, *United States Security Strategy for the East Asia-Pacific Region*, February 1995.

33 Richard N. Haass, *The Opportunity: America's Moment to Alter History's Course*, Public Affairs, New York, 2005, p. 147. Also, in the same book, Haass said that an effective multilateralism is based on keeping a respectful distance from the core interest of other major powers. A number of factors will affect the behaviour of other governments when it comes to associating themselves with US leadership, including the extent to which the United States is responsive to their concerns when their vital interests are in play.

34 Ashton B. Carter and William J. Perry, 'China on the March', *National Interest*, March/April 2007, p. 17.

35 *China's National Defense in 2006*, Information Office of the State Council of the People's Republic of China, available at <http://www.china.org.cn/english/features/book/194421.htm>, accessed 5 May 2008. See also Richard N. Haass, *The Opportunity: America's Moment to Alter History's Course*.

36 Nan Huaijing, one of the most respected scholars in China, has quoted this saying.

37 Arnold Toynbee, *Mankind and Mother Earth: A Narrative History of the World*, Oxford University Press, New York, 1976.

38 Translated by the author from Xong Shili, *Tenet for Reading Classical Chinese (Du Jing Shi Yao)*, The Chinese People University Press, Beijing, 2006.

39 J. William Fulbright, *The Price of Empire*, Pantheon Books, New York, 1989, p. 232.

40 Carter and Perry, 'China on the March', p. 16.

41 *Forging a world of Liberty Under Law: U.S. National Security Strategy for the 21st Century*.

42 Haass, *The Opportunity: America's Moment to Alter History's Course*, pp. 17, 22, 26, 32 and 202.

43 Donald W. White, *The American Century: the Rise and Decline of the United States as a World Power*, Yale University Press, New Haven, CT, 1996, p. 438.

Chapter 9

Potential Strategic Risks in China-US Relations

Yuan Peng

There is no denying the fact that the current China-US relationship is enjoying the best of times: reciprocal interests are deeply interwoven, a variety of mechanisms have been set up in succession and a fine trend of constructive cooperation is in progress. However, a cool-headed analysis reveals that, at present, the stability in the China-US relationship is tactical rather than strategic. The potential strategic risks should never be discounted considering the great differences between the social systems and ideologies of the two nations, potential clashes between the rising power and the status quo hegemon, growing collisions between geopolitics and geo-economics, and the diametrically opposed stance on the Taiwan issue which remains unsettled. Taking into consideration all these factors, this chapter intends to make a brief evaluation of those risks that will affect the strategic stability of China-US relations into the future.

From a holistic perspective, the most fundamental risk in China-US relations consists in the overall collision of China's rapid rise and all-round integration into the international system with the global interests of the United States. A primary feature of the China-US relationship is that it is comprehensive, strategic and global. This feature determines that it is unlikely that the two nations will wage war against each other given the compelling interests that each has at stake. Nevertheless, since the relationship between the two nations involves conflict of interest, the odds are extremely high for them to generate frictions on all counts. China will achieve a sustainable momentum in its development during the next decade, will become a member of the international community in a more profound way and play its due role in the construction of the international system. As a result, conflicts are bound to arise between China and the United States as the leader of the existing system. If handled inappropriately or not in time, these conflicts are prone to be turned into risks. Specifically speaking, there are altogether seven potential risks.

1. From a geopolitical point of view, the frictions between China and the United States during the next decade will mainly unfold in the Asia-Pacific region. The influence that both nations exert in the Asia-Pacific region must undergo a process of continuous checks and balances, in which risks may occur.

China is an acknowledged Asia-Pacific nation, but the United States has also always claimed itself to be an Asia-Pacific nation. There is an intense rivalry in geopolitics between the two nations. For a fairly long period after the Sino-Japanese War of 1894–95, China remained a weak and destitute power. Japan or the United States played a leading role in the order of the Asia-Pacific region and, for a time, they alternated in that role. Viewed from objective realities, competitiveness between China and the United States never took shape. However, the rapid rising of China is gradually changing this pattern, for China's initial rise proceeded in the Asia-Pacific region—the central arena of China's diplomacy. Although China had no intention of expanding its influence across the globe, it could not help but extend the rational development of economy and trade, and promote benefits from its diplomatic relations. Recently, China has made substantial headway in enhancing ties with member countries of the Association of Southeast Asian Nations (ASEAN), Middle Asia, Northeast Asia and even South Asia, which is indicative of an irresistible natural and historical trend for China to infiltrate its power into the Asia-Pacific region. In contrast, the United States got entangled in counter-terrorism and Middle East issues. Meanwhile, the misuse of strategy was undermining the dominant power of the United States in the Asia-Pacific region. In Northeast Asia, the growing gravity of the North Korean nuclear issue found the United States uncertain as to how to proceed, and the stronger dissonant tendency of South Korea was a hard nut for the United States to crack. On the surface, Japan showed a friendly gesture of cooperation, but virtually intended to take advantage of the US assistance to attain its own goal. The United States was fully aware of the real intention of Japan but could do nothing about it. Simultaneously, economic integration in the Northeast Asia region seemed to be in full swing without any hindrance from the political divergences. The United States had already sensed the great changes taking place in the historical pattern of the Northeast Asia region. Moreover, it witnessed the rapid rising of a mightier and influential China in the fact that China took the lead in the Six-Party Talks and facilitated its trade and economic cooperation with Japan and South Korea by considerable strides. In Southeast Asia, Thailand and the Philippines shared a totally different goal from their allied power—the United States—and their relationship with China seemed to gain an upper hand over that with the United States. The ASEAN influence represented by Islamic countries (such as Malaysia) was germinating a strong public sentiment against the United States. After the 1997–98 Asian financial crisis, ASEAN member countries were inclined to rely more on the rising power of China than on the blueprint of free trade advocated by the United States to revitalise their economies. A brand-new Southeast Asia was emerging on the horizon. What worried the United States more was that the 'China threat' once prevalent in the ASEAN countries was being substituted by the 'China opportunity'.

Obviously, the United States could not be reconciled with the loss of its dominance in the Asia-Pacific region, and spared no effort to consolidate, buttress and reinforce its controlling power over the region. If China wanted to rise in a smooth and steady way, it would be bound to further expand its influence in the Asia-Pacific region. How can this situation of manifest strategic competition be defused? For the time being, no effective solutions have emerged. On the contrary, misjudgement in strategic moves by both nations has been on the increase. The United States believes that China is now pursuing an Asian version of the 'Monroe doctrine', which is aimed at constructing a 'China in, America out' multilateral network to restore China as the Asian hegemon. On the part of China, the United States is seen as overtly or covertly building up a 'strategic ring of encirclement' in the hope of blocking China's rise. This strategic misjudgement is likely to touch off some sensitive issues and lead to antagonism between the two nations. Cases in point include the East China Sea issue between China and Japan, the China-US confrontation on the North Korean nuclear issue, and the fierce contest over multilateral mechanisms in East Asia. For China, the most testing policy challenge is how to continuously elevate its influence in the Asia-Pacific region while meticulously avoiding a head-on collision with the United States.

2. As regards resources and energy, a conflict is escalating between the increasing resources and energy demand of China and the control of the United States over the energy market. The risk in the energy conflict has become an inevitable reality.

For two decades since China's opening-up to the outside world, it has succeeded in materialising the rapid development of a national economy mainly dependent on its own resources and energy. Therefore, before entering into the twenty-first century, the conflict in resources and energy between China and the United States was not placed on the agenda. However, along with the acceleration of China's rise and the growing demand on resources and energy, as well as the energy diplomacy actively promoted by China in recent years with Latin America, Africa and the Middle East, the United States launched a sudden propaganda campaign over the so-called 'energy threat of China' and made the energy issue one of the primary concerns in the China-US strategic dialogues. As far as long-term development in China is concerned, the energy issue is bound to be a key factor affecting the China-US relationship over the longer term. In concrete terms, this risk comprises the following four aspects.

First, as the top two energy-consuming nations, China and the United States are on strategically competitive terms with each other. In order to strive for the global market, companies from both nations are undergoing keen competition which is liable to evoke potential friction. At the same time, the United States shows great anxiety over the increase of the international oil price ensuing from

China's soaring demand on energy resources. As was projected by several research institutions and financial service firms such as Morgan Stanley & Co., in 2020 China will have surpassed the United States and become the foremost energy consuming nation. In addition, according to the prediction of the International Energy Agency, China's petroleum imports will account for 75 per cent of the world's total demand for oil in 2020. Nowadays, 'energy threat of China' has turned out to be the most sonorous slogan in the West.

Second, there has been an upsurge of trade protectionism inside the United States, which has led to an inimical attitude toward China-US energy cooperation. Concerning the failure of the China National Offshore Oil Corporation (CNOOC)'s acquisition of UNOCAL, this move indicates that risks do exist for China-US relations: the acquisition of strategic resources could trigger tension in the political relationship.

Third, there is a clash in the energy diplomacy between China and the United States. As is stated in the book *China: the Balance Sheet—What the World Needs to Know About the Emerging Superpower*:

> Beijing is endeavoring to develop diplomatic relations with almost all countries who can export resources to China so as to help China ensure a smooth and sound functioning of her economic machines. This, more often than not, gives rise to the frequent friction between China and the United States in their diplomatic field, for China has established a close relationship with some unpopular regimes.[1]

Sudan's Darfur crisis has become one of the leading issues affecting China-US strategic relations. While this appears to be a collision of diplomatic principles between the two nations, it actually reflects the fact that China, in the context of its increasing demand for energy resources, is giving strategic priority to developing energy cooperation with countries such as Iran, Venezuela, Myanmar, and Nigeria, many of which have antagonistic relations with the United States. On the other hand, the United States deems that the energy diplomacy adopted by China will change the latter's relationship with Russia, Middle Asia and Japan in some measure, thus calling forth new variables in the international political order.

Fourth, risks can be found in the safety of energy pathways. Since 90 per cent of China's imported petroleum is transported via offshore oil tankers, China will develop its naval and marine policies accordingly. According to analysts from the United States, China will take greater initiatives in protecting its own energy supply, including the development of its 'blue-water' naval power and the construction of overland pipelines spanning South Asia, Southeast Asia, Middle Asia, and Northeast Asia. All these measures taken by the Chinese Government are certain to impact on the strategic interests of the United States.

In the absence of necessary strategic communication and cooperation between the two nations, further suspicion and misunderstanding are prone to cause risks.

3. From the perspective of diplomacy, the risk in China-US relations is mainly focused on how China will treat those countries that the United States, under the recent Bush Administration, characterised as so-called 'rogue states'. Such nations included North Korea, Iran, Venezuela, Pakistan, Sudan, Myanmar, Nepal, Nigeria, Syria and Cuba. Now that the basic strategy adopted by the United States towards China has already steered from exaggerating the so-called 'China threat' to exhorting 'China's responsibility', how China deals with 'the most irresponsible' states or governments in the world will be regarded as the touchstone to test whether China is willing to be a 'responsible stakeholder' as the United States has proposed. This poses a dual challenge or risk for China's diplomacy.

The first challenge or risk lies in forcing China to 'choose one side on which to stand'. The abovementioned nations, defined as 'rogue states' by the United States, have always been treated as normal developing countries or even as 'quasi-allies' in China's diplomatic framework. Over a long time, based on factors such as ideology, historical tradition, social system and political interests, China has been fostering friendly cooperation with them, and meanwhile seeking to also develop trade and strategic relations with the United States. Nevertheless, with China's gradual integration with the Western world and the deepening of the constructive and cooperative aspects of the China-US relationship, China's strategy of 'considering both sides' has outlived its usefulness and faces weightier pressure, for the United States has already sent out an explicit signal for China to 'choose one side'. However, if China turns a cold shoulder to these countries and facilitates China-US relations unreservedly, it will be caught up in a situation of 'easy to abandon, hard to resume' and experience deteriorating relations with those countries. If China sticks to its usual practice—developing a parallel relationship with both the United States and those countries—China would surely be subjected to powerful pressure from the interior politics of the United States, thereby affecting the next move in the development of China-US relations. This is therefore a dilemma for China's diplomacy.

The second challenge or risk is in urging China to forsake the principle of 'non-interference in others' internal affairs'. The pressure from the United States is not only confined to asking China to 'choose one side', but is also aimed at urging China to make due intervention in the internal affairs of those nations. As wished by the United States, the 'peaceful collapse' of Kim Jong-il's regime might materialise through China-US cooperation; while the Sudanese Government could be overturned and the Burmese regime could be reformed with an active role played by the Chinese Government. If China turns a deaf ear to these well-advised proposals, it will continue to encounter political pressures from the United States and put its diplomacy at a disadvantage. If China did act, the 'non-interference' principle in its diplomatic relations would be shaken and toppled. In the United States, the view is already widely held that China's attitude toward the North Korean nuclear issue can be considered as the embodiment of 'interference in the internal affairs of other nations'.

The risks and dilemma mentioned above have obliged China's foreign policy community to assess carefully whether China should review its diplomatic concepts or determine that retaining the primacy of 'non-interference' continues to serve China's interests.

4. From the aspect of society system and ideology, there is a risk of a 'China model' shock on the 'America model'. As noted American strategist Joseph S. Nye, Jr. pointed out in 'The Rise of China's Soft Power', 'although China is far from America's equal in soft power, it would be foolish to ignore the gains it is making'.[2] Nye's view represents a widespread concern in America that the 'China model' might in fact become competitive with the American one. In the United States, the 'China model' is labelled as 'totalitarianism + market economy + soft diplomacy'. The United States has two concerns. First, the 'China model' directly 'shocks' the American model. After the Cold War, the United States spoke of 'the end of history', and considered the American liberal democracy model as having triumphed over its main rival. But, in recent years, it has gradually realised that the specific Chinese developing model not only has strong vitality in China, but also holds a special attraction for a number of states further afield. Especially at a time when the United States is in a broader strategic predicament, the sudden rise of the China model is viewed as something of a threat. Second, it indirectly 'shocks' the America model. It does so by providing an 'alternative choice' to those countries at a strategic crossroads, thereby causing some to incline to the China model, and to objectively block the US grand strategy of propelling freedom and democracy. Thus, as can be seen, the 'debate on the model' is fundamentally important to the United States. To counteract the shock of the China model, the United States is certain to increase the global infiltration of its soft power, or to choose to decry the expansion of Chinese culture so as to elevate the issue to the level of the global expansion of Chinese ideology and even of China's strategic design, leading to new perceptions of a 'China threat' worldwide. Once this occurs, it will become more difficult for China to maintain and extend its period of strategic opportunities.

5. From the aspect of domestic stability, China is faced with two risks: the interference and even fluctuation of both its economic base and its social base. At present, it seems that the risk of political confrontation and military conflict taking place between China and the United States is relatively low, because of a deep blending of China and the United States. The United States, however,

although changing its strategies and areas of emphasis, has never given up on transforming, guiding and modelling China; that is, from overturning China's political base to loosening China's social base, and from direct military restraint to undermining China's economic base.

On the one hand, the United States enhances its influence over China's social fabric via concealed but legal channels such as non-governmental organisations (NGOs) and religious infiltration. A central idea of the so-called 'Transformational Diplomacy' that former US Secretary of State Condoleezza Rice intimated in early 2006 was for US embassy staffs and NGO members to go deep inside the societies of targeted countries, not least, China. Since China is in a period of social transformation, there is an intricate array of social tensions that offer opportunities for US infiltration. The United States has seized these opportunities and is on its way toward a new 'Peaceful Transformation' in a planned and systematic way. More and more think-tank scholars are putting their emphasis on social fields such as local elections, community events, socially vulnerable groups, environment destruction, health issues (e.g., Acquired Immune Deficiency Syndrome), immigration, the income gap, and state enterprise reformation. Their research paves the way for the development of government policy. Many NGO members with backgrounds in government have also shifted their working emphasis to these fields; they 'strive for people's support with the Communist Party' and even visit the poor. Their activities have a very strong influence among the Chinese at the grass-roots level. Meanwhile, religious groups carry out infiltration of all forms, taking advantage of underground churches and of any loosening up in China's religious policy. The abovementioned methods are not easy for the Chinese Government to deal with, since the United States Government is not directly involved and because such groups and organisations reach into every corner of Chinese society in the name of charity or research. If China controls it too strictly, the government could be viewed as blocking NGO activity; but if it lets such organisations do as they like, it could all too easily cause 'boiled frog syndrome'. And once such NGOs have enough effect at the grass-roots level, they might potentially endanger China's social superstructure.

On the other hand, the United States enhances its strength through interference in China's economic base. A prominent American economic target has been the state enterprise, which is the lifeline and foundation of China's economic development. For example, in the author's opinion, the 2006 acquisition of Xugong Group by the Carlyle Group indicated that the United States was ready to take a significant shareholding in China's large state enterprises. From the US standpoint, while it has coped reasonably well with the challenges (especially intellectual property protection and an undervalued Yuan) from China's small and medium-sized enterprises, it does not seem to have found an effective way to cope with the state enterprises. The United States is going to make full use of two methods in the future. The first is to encourage market opening and further economic reform, followed by a gradual encroachment on China's large-sized state enterprises. The second method is via the financial insurance industry, which is part of the so-called tertiary industry sector. Since the reform and opening-up, the United States has focused on China's economy in three consecutive waves. The first wave came before China's entry into the World Trade Organization (WTO). Its key objective was to exert pressure on China's primary industry (essentially its agricultural products)—a goal that the United States considers it by and large achieved. The second wave came after China's entry into the WTO, when the focus shifted to China's industry (especially textile and manufacturing), and the instruments included criticising China's Renminbi (RMB) exchange rate, its mercantilist export-oriented economic model, its failure to protect workers' rights and interests and so on. At present, the United States considers that it has made useful progress on this front. In the future, it will concentrate on China's tertiary industry, especially the financial insurance industry, which is a highly specialised industry but one that touches the entire economy. More importantly, it is America's strength in international competition and its time-tested 'unique dagger' which interferes so effectively with the economic lifeline of developing countries. The United States Government chose its then Secretary of the Treasury, Henry Paulson, to take the lead in opening the China-US strategic economic dialogue, and placed the opening-up of the financial sector at centre stage in this dialogue. It would be prudent for China to be thoughtful and vigilant about US intentions.

In sum, the United States has focused on China's two weak points (its social base and its economic base) and has engaged in activities that, while seemingly peaceful, actually have strategic intent. It is one of the most difficult risks for China to deal with in the future.

6. From the aspect of crisis management, the Taiwan issue is still the highest risk. Although the Taiwan issue is temporally in a controllable state, China-US cooperation on avoiding a sprint to independence is limited. The structural conflicts between China and the United States still reside in some fundamental problems on this front. First, the basis of America's 'one China' policy is not reliable. Not only is the connotation different from the 'one China principle' that China sticks to, voices in both the US Congress and in conservative think-tanks have often clamoured in recent times for the abandonment of the 'one China' position. If the Taiwan issue changes significantly, the United States will probably make an issue of the 'one China principle' and demand more concessions from China for its retention. Second, the 'Dual Containment Policy' policy of the United States, which keeps Taiwan from risking 'instant independence' and restrains the Mainland from non-peaceful ways to resolve the issue, has not changed. Thus, the United States can carry on its counter-balancing policy, manipulating the ups and downs of the Taiwan issue. If China ever endeavoured to resolve the Taiwan issue in its own way, it would

inevitably lead to serious confrontation and conflict with the United States. Third, the US policy on arms sales to Taiwan is becoming more dangerous. It seems to the author that the United States has shown scant regard for the '8.17 Communiqué', and US-Taiwan military transactions have become more open, with the two sides even bargaining transparently in the presence of the Mainland. If this trend is not curbed in time, the danger is obvious. Fourth, the United States has not changed its strategy that positions Taiwan as a factor to contain or influence the future direction of China. From the standpoint of containment, US-Taiwan military cooperation has reached the equivalent of a 'non-NATO ally'—a relatively select category—and has transitioned from hardware to software. In the arena of theatre missile defence, the basic US strategy is to treat its regional partners as part of a trinity: the United States, as a command centre; Japan, as a launching platform, and Taiwan as an intelligence-gathering outpost. The US purpose is to deny the Mainland any option to use force against Taiwan and to blunt Beijing's capacity to bring China's comprehensive national strength to bear, thus preserving the status of the Taiwan Strait as one of 'neither war nor peace', of 'neither unification nor independence'. In broader terms, the United States hopes Taiwan can play a role as a model of democracy, and ultimately lead the Mainland towards democratisation.

The next two years constitute a high-risk period for the Taiwan issue. First, there has been a notable increase in US arms sales to Taiwan. China's reaction to any such development will directly shape the direction of the current China–US–Taiwan interaction. Second, the United States and Taiwan entered their election countdowns in 2007, with changes in leadership by 2009.[3] Taiwan is likely to go on making an issue of reunification and independence. The possibility of Taiwan's President Chen Shui-bian exploiting the Mainland's pre-occupation with hosting the 2008 Summer Olympic Games and openly taking risks for constitutional amendment could be ruled out.

7. From the aspect of military conflict, the West Pacific region and outer space are potential high-risk areas for China-US military conflict. The risks should not be ignored. Although China-US political ties gradually stabilised in 2007, the lack of mutual trust in the military sphere is still evident and, in fact, may have worsened in some respects. The response by the US Congress and the media to China's Anti-Satellite Missile Test was a case in point. The hearings of the US–China Economic and Security Review Commission of Congress held on 1 February 2007, and commentary in the *Washington Post* and other mainstream media supposedly decrying those 'taken in' by the notion of China's peaceful rise, was another.

In fact, China-US military relations, despite a great degree of recovery, have to cope with very different perspectives and even contradictory objectives. In the eyes of the United States, China's military modernisation should be transparent and also limited. The desired limits preclude expansion onto the high seas and into outer space. The United States regards sea power and air power as the lifeline of its military strategy and any Chinese militarisation at sea (especially into the West Pacific) or in space is taboo in US eyes. Contradictions and even conflicts will be unavoidable in these circumstances. Therefore, preventing confrontations between the armed forces in the West Pacific region and in space constitutes a serious problem for China-US relations that will have to be addressed in the near future.

In recent years, the United States has made it clear that it regards the West Pacific region as its exclusive domain, and an arena in which China's military forces should not meddle. In 2006, China's military authorities were invited to observe the largest joint military exercises held in the region since the Vietnam War. This invitation appeared to be intended as a warning. The United States has repeatedly hinted that it does not care about China's development of its ground forces, but is resolutely opposed to the expansion of China's naval power. Therefore, 'punitive actions' directed at China's military power, and the generation of small-scale crises, led by the United States alone (or with Japan, in the Western Pacific region, such as the 'aircraft collision incident' off Hainan on 1 April 2001), cannot be ruled out.

ENDNOTES

[1] C. Fred Bergsten, Bates Gill, Nicholas R. Lardy and Derek Mitchell, *China: The Balance Sheet: What the World Needs to Know About the Emerging Superpower*, Public Affairs, New York, 2006.

[2] Joseph S. Nye Jr., 'The Rise of China's Soft Power', opinion column in the *Wall Street Journal Asia*, 29 December 2005, available at
<http://belfercenter.ksg.harvard.edu/publication/1499/rise_of_chinas_soft_power.html>, accessed 17 June 2009.

[3] On 22 March 2008, Nationalist Party candidate Ma Ying-jeou was elected President of Taiwan. On 4 November 2008, Barack Obama became President-elect of the United States. He was inaugurated on 20 January 2009.

Chapter 10

Changes in China-Japan Relations and East Asian Security

Zhang Tuosheng

China-Japan relations have been turbulent for over a decade and endured a sustained deterioration in the political and security fields, especially from 2001 to 2006. The bilateral relationship finally made a major turn towards a new stage of development, marked by Japanese Prime Minister Shinzo Abe's ice-breaking visit to China and Premier Wen Jiabao's ice-melting journey to Japan. Changes and developments in China-Japan relations will exert a profound and far-reaching influence over East Asian security.

China-Japan relations have actually witnessed remarkable growth since their normalisation in 1972. However, due to deep changes in the international situation and within both countries, China-Japan relations entered a prolonged period of turbulence in the mid-1990s.[1] During that period, frictions increased and intensified continuously. With complete suspension of high-level contact at the end of 2005, bilateral relations fell to rock bottom. Serious deterioration of China-Japan relations not only directly undermined the strategic interests of both countries, but also caused serious international concern.

With efforts from both sides, Abe visited China in October 2006. The two sides reached important common understandings, including (1) working together to overcome political barriers and comprehensively promoting bilateral relations; (2) resuming exchanges and dialogue between leaders; (3) correctly appraising the other's path to development; (4) accelerating consultation on the joint development of disputed territories in the East China Sea; and (5) constructing a mutually beneficial relationship based on common strategic interests. The visit served to break the political stalemate between the two countries, thus opening the gate to further improvement and development of bilateral relations.

Premier Wen Jiabao visited Japan in April 2007, the first visit by a Chinese premier in seven years. The two sides agreed further on properly handling major differences and reached a consensus on the basic spirit and content of a mutually beneficial strategic relationship as well as on some measures to begin to develop this new relationship. Premier Wen's speech at the Japanese Diet was widely welcomed. The visit also opened the 35th anniversary celebration of normalisation of relations and instituted the China-Japan Culture and Sports Exchange Year. The successful visit by Premier Wen consolidated the improvements in bilateral relations since October 2006, registering a solid step towards establishing strategic mutually beneficial relations. The major turn in China-Japan relations is manifested in three areas.

First, the two sides agreed on resolving the question of the Yasukuni Shrine and found a pragmatic solution.[2] This was a key step in breaking the political stalemate that had been formed because of the then Japanese Prime Minister Junichiro Koizumi's visits to the Shrine during the previous five years. Many people find the agreement still rather fragile. However, I believe it was a decision made after careful thought on both sides rather than an act of expediency. Given that differences over history are hard to resolve definitively in the short term, it serves the interests of both sides to prevent them damaging the wider bilateral relationship. Furthermore, China has already demonstrated to Japan, and continues to show, that it has no intention of playing the history card. Facts will gradually dispel misgivings on the part of the Japanese public.[3] The possibility that Abe would resume visits to the Shrine to reverse adverse political developments ahead of lower House elections in July 2007 was remote.[4] Improved relations with China represented one of Abe's major achievements and enjoyed extensive domestic support. Why would he have made such a self-defeating move?

Second, the two sides agreed to resume and strengthen high-level exchanges, and remarkable progress has been made in this regard. In today's world, particularly where major countries are concerned, high-level exchanges are a basic condition for the development of normal state-to-state relations. On this basis, certain mutual trust between major leaders may play a uniquely positive role in facilitating the improvement and development of relations between their countries. However, for quite some time, the steady worsening of China-Japan relations seriously obstructed high-level contact, which became the weakest link in bilateral ties. Remarkable changes took place after October 2006. Major leaders met on three international occasions and realised the first exchange of visits. Then an exchange of visits between Prime Minister Abe and President Hu Jintao was placed on the agenda. Resumption and strengthening of high-level contact is a substantive part of the major turn in the relationship and will play a key role in consolidating improvements and preventing any reversal.

Third, the two sides reached common understandings on establishing a mutually beneficial strategic relationship, which reset the baseline of bilateral relations on common interest. About four years ago, this author analysed the reasons for the worsening of relations between China and Japan and found that, apart from the direct causes of disputes over history, Taiwan and the East China Sea, this deterioration had more profound roots: the end of the Cold War and the appearance of a relationship between two major Asian powers. Neither side was prepared or accustomed to such a situation, which led to increasing friction and a relationship dominated by differences.[5] The idea of jointly establishing a mutually beneficial strategic relationship marked a major change in mindset and a new starting point in establishing political mutual trust. It indicates the determination of both sides to seek common ground while shelving differences and placing common interests at the top of their agenda. By so doing, the two major powers are abandoning the old idea of 'no two rival tigers on the same mountain' and starting to work together for cooperation and a 'win–win' situation.

With these three changes, China-Japan exchanges and cooperation turned warmer, growing and strengthening in many fields. The two sides strengthened cooperation on resolving the North Korean nuclear issue and maintaining stability on the Korean Peninsula. China also expressed a willingness to offer possible assistance to Japan on the kidnapping question, which was welcomed by Japan. Negotiations on the joint development of the East China Sea sped up and entered into the stage of discussing detailed schemes for joint development. Japan expressed its understanding of China's serious concern over the question of Taiwan, reaffirmed its commitment to the three political documents, and to its undertaking not to support Taiwan independence. A joint research program on the history question, guided by both governments, was formally launched and two workshops were held. Military relations achieved a new momentum with the Chinese Defence Minister visiting Japan and an exchange of naval visits was planned. Exchanges between political parties of the two countries as well as between the Chinese National People's Congress and the Japanese Diet became more active. The two sides also launched high-level economic dialogue and energy policy dialogue mechanisms. Together with the 35th anniversary celebrations and the launch of a series of events under the Year of Cultural and Sport Exchanges, non-governmental exchanges also gained momentum.

This major turning point in China-Japan relations has not been accidental, but rather is driven by a sense of necessity.

First, the continued worsening of relations had seriously damaged the strategic interests of both countries. Over the previous seven years, various disputes had surfaced, public sentiments had become increasingly confrontational and mutual strategic suspicions had grown strong.[6] With the outbreak of large-scale anti-Japan demonstrations in some Chinese cities in 2005, people began to worry that the situation of 'cold politics and warm economy'[7] between China and Japan could move towards 'cold politics and cold economy', which would lead to unthinkable prospects. To break the political stalemate and to guide bilateral relations towards stability and improvement gradually became a desire of both countries.

Furthermore, the worsening of China-Japan relations caused much concern in the international community. Poor China-Japan relations not only weakened their cooperation in establishing regional multilateral cooperation mechanisms such as the ASEAN Plus Three (APT) and the East Asia Summit (EAS), but also increased difficulty in reforming the United Nations Security Council (UNSC) and led to a serious imbalance in the China–US–Japan triangle. No country in East Asia wishes to be forced to make a choice between China and Japan. Although the United States has never wanted to see the level of the China-Japan relationship approaching or even exceeding that of the US-China or US-Japan relationships, worsening China-Japan relations embody the danger of confrontation between the US-Japan alliance and China and of increased difficulty in coordination and cooperation between the US-South Korea alliance and the US-Japan alliance, with both Koreas holding a historical view of Japan similar to that of China. Moreover, although the United States Government has long been reluctant to publicly criticise the revisionist historical view in Japan, the growing salience of the Yasukuni Shrine problem and consequent rising criticism from the US Congress and the strategic studies community pushed the Bush Administration into an awkward position. The international community, including the United States, had become eager to see stability and improvement in China-Japan relations at an early date.

Additionally, ever since 2005, the two governments (China in particular) had been attempting to break the political stalemate and improve bilateral relations. A meeting between Chinese President Hu Jintao and the then Japanese Prime Minister, Junichiro Koizumi, in Indonesia in April 2005,[8] which led to the start of strategic dialogue and the resumption of negotiations over the East China Sea in the following month, had sparked hope. The Chinese Government gave a positive comment on Koizumi's statement in commemorating the sixtieth anniversary of the Second World War. Even after the two sides' efforts were once again stalled by Koizumi's visit to the Yasukuni Shrine, contacts continued in the most difficult circumstances in 2006, with exchanges between the two ruling parties, a Foreign Ministers' meeting, strategic dialogue,[9] East China Sea negotiations, people-to-people dialogue and Track 2 dialogue. At the same time, China began to release positive signals[10] towards future Japanese leaders. The most likely next Prime Minster, Abe, then Chief Cabinet Minister, began to adopt ambiguity over Yasukuni Shrine.[11] Finally, the two sides seized the opportunity of a Japanese leadership change and agreed (through arduous negotiation) on overcoming political barriers and promoting healthy development of friendly and cooperative relations, leading to the long-awaited turn in bilateral relations.

However, the foundation for the turn is still rather fragile. The three major friction points (Taiwan, history, and the East China Sea) remain. The serious confrontation in public sentiments that have formed during the continuous worsening of bilateral relations will remain difficult to manage, and take time to reverse. At a more profound level, the mutual strategic suspicion will not disappear overnight.[12]

In this situation, in order that progress can be made in building a mutually beneficial strategic relationship, it should be a paramount task for China and Japan to fully consolidate and expand the opening that has been created and strive to make the turn for the better irreversible. The two sides must stick unswervingly to the common understanding of jointly eliminating political barriers, and to properly handling the history issue and placing it appropriately so as to prevent it from becoming, yet again, a major barrier to the development of bilateral relations. At the same time, efforts should be made to maintain and further develop high-level exchanges on a regular and institutionalised basis and in diversified forms, making it among the most important mechanisms to promote bilateral relations and to control and handle bilateral differences.

The two sides must be aware that it will not be smooth sailing in the quest to improve bilateral relations. Problems may arise from time to time and frictions may resurface in various forms. Some questions, if not properly handled, may even incur serious damage to bilateral relations. With the March 2008 'presidential' election in Taiwan drawing near, the question of Taiwan may well gain prominence and should attract serious attention from both sides.[13] All in all, at present and in the coming one to two years, it is essential to properly and prudently handle various differences between the countries, including possible new differences.[14]

While continuing to control and narrow differences and consolidate existing gains and benefits, the two sides must seize the opportunity to rapidly expand cooperation and promote development of mutually beneficial strategic relations. This will be the key to whether China-Japan relations may have a new future. Since October 2006, through repeated discussions, China and Japan have already reached three very important points of common understanding in this regard.

First, the basic spirit of mutually beneficial strategic relations has been set; that is, jointly making constructive contribution to peace, stability and development in Asia and the whole world through bilateral, regional and international cooperation, and in that process benefiting each other, expanding common interest and pushing bilateral relations to a new high.[15] This basic spirit goes beyond differences and places mutual benefit and expanded common interest in a paramount position. It also goes beyond bilateral cooperation and expands the foundation of bilateral relations to broader areas of regional and international cooperation. Such a spirit will be of long-term significance in guiding the effort to construct a mutually beneficial strategic relationship.

Second, the basic contents of a mutually beneficial strategic relationship have been clarified. They include: (1) supporting each other's peaceful development and increasing mutual political trust; (2) deepening mutually beneficial cooperation and realising common development; (3) strengthening defence dialogue and exchanges and working together for regional stability; (4) increasing cultural and personnel exchanges and promoting mutual understanding and friendly sentiments between the two peoples; and (5) enhancing coordination and cooperation in a joint effort to deal with regional and global issues.[16] The basic contents touch upon varying levels of China-Japan relations, provide a clearly drawn blueprint for the construction of a mutually beneficial strategic relationship and identify the direction in which the many dimensions of the relationship must move. Among all these contents, the first one is of guiding significance and constitutes a foundation for mutually beneficial strategic relations.

Third, practical steps have been identified, such as comprehensively improving and strengthening various bilateral dialogue and exchange mechanisms including high-level contacts, strengthening mutually beneficial cooperation in nine areas (including areas such as energy, environmental protection, information and communication technology, and finance), and focusing on strengthened cooperation on regional and international affairs (including, in particular, reform of the United Nations and the Six-Party Talks).[17] Many of these steps are in the nature of recovering a badly depleted relationship. However, there are also specific cooperation measures, such as the launch of high-level economic dialogue, exchange of naval visits, strengthened defence liaison, increased energy and intellectual property rights cooperation and more dialogue on UN reform, which are of ground-breaking significance for bilateral relations. Furthermore, China made it clear that it is 'ready to see a greater and constructive role played by Japan in international affairs'.[18] This is another important sign, which will have a far-reaching influence over future China-Japan cooperation in international relations.

Constructing a mutually beneficial strategic relationship is an arduous task that will take time to accomplish. The two sides need to translate their common understanding into action. Culturally, China values the overall situation and principles while Japan treasures details and tangible benefits. The two sides should be aware of their cultural differences and make the effort to adapt to and complement each other. They need to set their eyes on the long-term and overall interests but start with minor actions and with a flexible and pragmatic attitude, thereby promoting bilateral relations in a step-by-step and stable manner. So long as the two sides honour their commitment, act in line with their common understanding and work conscientiously together, the vision of a mutually beneficial strategic relationship between China and Japan can finally be realised.

Continued improvement and development of China-Japan relations will have a positive influence on East Asian security. First of all, it facilitates cooperation on the Six-Party Talks. With the continuous escalation of the North Korean nuclear crisis in 2006, people were worried about greater difficulty in coordination between China on the one hand and the United States and Japan on the other due to poor China-Japan relations and the more intense situation on the Korean Peninsula once North Korea carried out its first nuclear test. However, major changes in China-Japan relations exerted a positive influence over the development of the North Korean nuclear issue. After North Korea's nuclear test, the UNSC quickly adopted a resolution to impose sanctions on North Korea and the Six-Party Talks resumed shortly thereafter to register important progress. Admittedly, the positive developments on the North Korean nuclear issue had multiple causes, but improved China-Japan relations and strengthened cooperation between China, South Korea and Japan were certainly among them. Some people even believed that Japan sought to improve its relations with China partly out of its serious concern over the Korean Peninsula. This analysis makes sense. In the future, with China and Japan giving priority to the Six-Party Talks in their effort to develop regional and international cooperation, the positive effects of improved China-Japan relations will become more apparent.

Improved China-Japan relations have also helped to relax tensions over the East China Sea and to facilitate a peaceful resolution of the outstanding territorial and maritime disputes that are still widespread in East Asia. When state-to-state relations worsen, disputes over territory or maritime interests are not only difficult to resolve but may also trigger military conflict. In 2005, frictions over rival claims in the East China Sea developed to a dangerous level, with a marked increase in military surveillance by both China and Japan, more radical opinions in the confrontational national sentiments, and the appearance of the view that there would definitely be a war between China and Japan. Later, following negotiations, the two sides reached initial understandings on the common development of these disputed territories and the situation relaxed to some extent. Nonetheless, against the backdrop of a generally tense bilateral relationship, registering further progress will be very difficult and the risk of reversal is ever-present. Improvement in bilateral relations has created the necessary condition for common development of the East China Sea, allowing the two governments to gradually dispel disruptive nationalistic sentiments and find practical ways forward through sustained and serious dialogue and mutual compromise. After late 2006, the two sides increased their contact over the East China Sea issue. Their common understanding grew and they agreed to strive for a specific scheme of common development to be reported to leaders of the two countries in the fall of 2007.[19] If China and Japan are successful in jointly developing their claims in the East China Sea, they will not only create conditions for the two sides to resolve their maritime boundary dispute and the Diaoyutai Islands dispute in the future, but also set a positive example for other countries in the region in relaxing tension and resolving disputes over territory or maritime interests.

Moreover, improved China-Japan relations are conducive to maintaining peace and stability across the Taiwan Strait, which serves the interests of the Mainland, Taiwan and others in East Asia (including Japan), as well as those nations outside the region (such as the United States). However, the development of pro-independence forces in Taiwan constitutes a huge challenge to peace and stability in the region. In recent years, with the sustained stable development of China-US relations, their cooperation to prevent Taiwan-independence sentiments disrupting the status quo has increased and their friction over the Taiwan question has decreased. However, frictions between China and Japan over Taiwan have been on the rise due to the worsening relationship. Pro-Taiwan forces in Japan have gained influence, official contacts with Taiwan have increased, and Japan's Taiwan policy has moved from one of ambiguity to more clarity.[20] This has been exploited by Taiwan's independence forces. They even publicly called for the establishment of a quasi-military alliance with Japan against China. The worsening of China-Japan relations added complexity and risk to the situation in the Taiwan Strait. Any improvement and development in China-Japan relations may lead to increased cooperation between the two countries in maintaining peace and stability in the Taiwan Strait, thus containing the expansion of the Taiwan independence force and leaving China, the United States and Japan more space in which to manoeuvre in the event that the pro-independence forces provoke a crisis. The May 2007 US-Japan Security Consultative Committee (2 plus 2) meeting did not again list the peace and stability of the Taiwan Strait among its common strategic objectives, giving a positive signal[21] and helping to restrict the capacity of the pro-independence forces to disrupt the status quo in the Taiwan Strait.

Further, improved China-Japan relations will facilitate the establishment and development of a regional multilateral security cooperation mechanism. At present, East Asian security mechanisms are mainly composed of two parts: the US-led bilateral military alliances; and the rapidly developing bilateral and multilateral security dialogues in which coordination and cooperation among major powers play an important role. As time passes, the role of the ASEAN Regional Forum (ARF), the APT, the EAS and the Six-Party Talks will increase and that of bilateral military alliances will gradually decrease. In this process, improvement and development of China-Japan relations and strengthened military relations and defence dialogue will not only facilitate the formation of a relatively stable and coordinated triangular relationship between China, the United States and Japan; it will also create the conditions necessary for dialogue between China and the US-Japan alliance. Continued development of China-Japan relations will inject vigour into, and lay down the foundation for, the development of multilateral security mechanisms in East Asia. History will prove that only once China and Japan achieve a genuine reconciliation, and are able to cooperate comprehensively, can East Asia establish an effective multilateral security cooperation mechanism.

Finally, the continued improvement and development of China-Japan relations will also greatly enhance their cooperation in the fields of non-traditional security, such as counter-terrorism, guarding against financial and energy crises, treatment of environmental pollution and ecological destruction, prevention and treatment of international infectious diseases, combating transnational crime, and supplying international humanitarian assistance. Since the end of the Cold War, an important trend in the international situation has been the rise of non-traditional security challenges. Strengthened cooperation in this regard will be a necessary choice for China, Japan and other East Asian countries.

ENDNOTES

[1] With the end of the Cold War, both China-US relations and China-Japan relations experienced turbulence. China-US relations moved out of the 12-year turbulent period (1989–2001) and entered into a stage of relatively stable development, while the turbulent period of China-Japan relations, started in 1994, had (by 2006) also lasted for 12 years.

[2] Japan was to adopt a policy of ambiguity, while China was to drop its insistence on Japanese leaders' public commitment of not paying tribute to the Yasukuni Shrine. The Joint Press Communiqué issued on 8 October 2006 vowed to 'properly handle issues that affect development of bilateral relations and enable strong movement of both political and economic wheels'.

[3] The long-held opinion in Japan has been that China always plays the history card with Japan and that, even when the Yasukuni Shrine problem is resolved, China will take on other historical issues. Influenced by such a school of thought, many Japanese people, although not in favour of Koizumi visiting the Yasukuni Shrine, were either silent or supportive of his visit against the backdrop of an intense China-Japan dispute.

[4] Shinzo Abe resigned on 12 September 2007, barely one year after becoming Japan's Prime Minister.

[5] Zhang Tuosheng, 'Ruhe Fazhan Zhong Ri Changqi Youhao Hezuo Guanxi (How to development a long-term friendly and cooperative relationship between China and Japan)', *Zhongguo Pinglun* (*China Review*), vol. 1, 2006, p. 10.

[6] In Japan, the Chinese military threat school of thought was prevalent. In China, the public was seriously concerned about the possibility of Japan pursuing a path to military power or even reviving militarism.

[7] Since 2001, even with continued tension in the political and security fields, economic relations between China and Japan had maintained fairly good growth. This was called 'cold politics and warm economy'.

[8] President Hu Jintao proposed a five-point proposal on improving and developing China-Japan relations. See *Xinhuanet Jakarta* report on 23 April 2005.

[9] The three rounds of strategic dialogues in February, July and September 2006 played an important role in the two sides' effort to break the political stalemate.

[10] In February 2006, while meeting seven friendly organisations from Japan, President Hu Jintao made it clear that 'so long as Japanese leaders clearly make a decision not to visit again the Yasukuni Shrine hosting Class A War Criminals, I would like to have dialogue and meeting with Japanese leaders on improving and developing China-Japan relations'. In August 2006, he made a similar statement to the new Japanese Ambassador Yuji Miyamoto on the occasion of the latter's presentation of credentials.

[11] It was rather eye-catching that, in the summer of 2006, Japanese Prime Minister Shinzo Abe adopted an attitude of neither confirming nor denying media reports about his visit to the Yasukuni Shrine in the previous Spring.

[12] An outstanding example in this regard is the then Japanese Prime Minister Shinzo Abe's public request during his visit to Europe in Spring 2007 that the European Union should not lift its arms embargo over China.

[13] On 22 March 2008, Nationalist Party candidate Ma Ying-jeou was elected President of Taiwan.

[14] The prospect of Japan revising its Constitution has already caused deep concern in China.

[15] China–Japan Joint Press Communiqué, 11 April 2007, available at <http://www.fmprc.gov.cn/eng/wjdt/2649/t311005.htm>, accessed 17 June 2009.

[16] China–Japan Joint Press Communiqué, 11 April 2007.

[17] China–Japan Joint Press Communiqué, 11 April 2007.

[18] China–Japan Joint Press Communiqué, 11 April 2007.

[19] China–Japan Joint Press Communiqué, 11 April 2007.

[20] In the past, Japan had long been reluctant to make a public statement about whether it would intervene in the event of a military conflict in the Taiwan Strait. However, with the worsening of China-Japan relations, voices publicly arguing for intervention, together with some voices within the United States, have been on the rise.

[21] China believes that the relevant countries should jointly maintain peace and stability in the Taiwan Strait, but firmly opposes armed intervention by the US-Japan alliance in a Taiwan Strait conflict on any ground. The complete text of the 1 May 2007 Joint Statement of the Security Consultative Committee, 'Alliance Transformation: Advancing United States-Japan Security and Defense Cooperation' can be found at <http://www.mofa.go.jp/region/n-america/us/security/scc/joint0705.html>, accessed 17 June 2009.

Index

Abe, Shinzo 63, 112, 114, 119n4, 119n11, 120n12
   and visit to China 7, 111
Acharya, Amitav 12
Afghanistan 4, 33–37, 41–42
Africa 39, 70, 95, 98n21, 103
aid 41, 47–48, 54–55, 59, 61, 102, 113
   humanitarian assistance 36, 54, 76, 95, 119
air power and aircraft 110
   F-16 *Fighting Falcon* 87
   F-22 *Raptor* 87
Albright, Madeleine 13
alliances 1, 5, 7–8, 63–65, 68, 72, 74, 76, 79–80, 90–91, 105, 109
   bilateral alliance 1, 7, 115
   military alliance 47, 50, 65, 90–94, 118
   trilateral alliance 18, 63
   US-Japan alliance 47, 50, 80, 114, 118, 120n21
   US-South Korea alliance 114
Allison, Graham 86
Asia-Pacific Economic Cooperation (APEC) 8, 16, 60–62
Asian and Pacific Council 11
'Asian Values', concept of 28
Association of Southeast Asia 11
Association of Southeast Asian Nations (ASEAN) 2–3, 8, 11–14, 18, 21–30, 31n2, 38, 62, 69, 102
   ASEAN Cebu Summit (January 2007) 24
   ASEAN Celebrity Group 25
   ASEAN Charter Report 24: *ASEAN Charter* 24–25
   ASEAN Economic Community 24
   ASEAN Plus One 22, 25, 27
   ASEAN Plus Six 25
   ASEAN Plus Ten 8
   ASEAN Plus Three (APT) 8, 15–16, 25, 62, 114, 118
   ASEAN Regional Forum (ARF) 3, 8, 11–15, 62, 64, 92, 118
   'ASEAN Way', concept of 28
Australia 8, 12, 15–18, 27–28, 30, 62–64, 68, 77, 97
   Australian Government 2, 15–18, 63–65, 97
   Australian Research Council 1

'balance of powers', concept of 21, 82–83, 91
Balkans 34
   Kosovo campaign (1999) 81
Barnett, Thomas 90
Bay of Bengal 77
Bell, Coral 82
Britain: *see* United Kingdom
Brzezinski, Zbigniew 83
buffer zones 4, 49, 52
Burma: *see* Myanmar
Bush, George H.W. 71–72
Bush, George W. 51, 74, 77, 86–87
   Bush Administration 53, 59, 74, 77, 82, 92, 105, 114

Carter, Ashton B. 93, 96
Chen Shui-bian 109
Cheney, Dick 69–73, 90–91
China 1–6, 22, 26–31, 34, 38–40, 47, 53–56, 59–65, 68–69, 78–79, 81–82, 85–86, 90–95, 97, 98n22, 101–109, 118–19, 119n6, 120, 120n21
   'aircraft collision incident' (Hainan), 1 April 2001 110
   and concept of 'China threat' 90, 102, 105–106
   and concept of 'harmonious world' 52–53
   and concept of 'reform and opening-up' 47–48, 52, 103, 108
   and concepts of 'peaceful development', 'peaceful rise' and 'Peaceful Transformation' 52, 80, 107, 109, 116
   and 'One China principle' 108
   anti-Japanese demonstrations in (2005) 113
   Beijing 1, 5, 7: 2008 Summer Olympic Games 109
   Central Committee on Foreign Affairs 52

Changbai Mountains in 55
China Foundation for International and Strategic Studies 1
China National Offshore Oil Corporation 104: UNOCAL 104
China-North Korea border region 55
China-Soviet border 33
China's foreign policy community 106
China's foreign relations: *see* various entries under relations
China's rise 1, 12, 17–18, 25–26, 30, 102–103
Chinese Communist Party 107: Chinese Communist Party's Central Committee (CCPCC) 52
Chinese Government 2–5, 7, 12, 16–18, 30, 45–46, 48, 51–54, 56, 60, 65, 80–81, 83, 104–105, 107, 109, 114: Ministry of Foreign Affairs 52
Chinese military 47, 80, 86, 92–94, 96–97, 109–110, 119n6: People's Liberation Army (PLA) 6
Chinese National People's Congress 113: 17th Party Congress 54
Chinese policy 8, 12, 14, 16, 25–26, 29–30, 33, 45–47, 51–56, 61, 64, 80–81, 92–95, 102–106, 108, 113–14, 117
containment of China 17, 108–109, 118
Hong Kong Special Administrative Region 69
Macau Special Administrative Region 60
Clinton, Hillary 6, 31n2
Clinton, William (Bill) 92
Clinton Administration 74–76, 81
Cold War 1–2, 7–8, 21–24, 27, 30, 34, 48–49, 67–73, 75, 80, 86–89, 96, 106, 112, 119, 119n1
command and control 75
communication 35, 50, 83, 105, 116
communications technology 116
communiqués 7, 109, 119n2
high-level contact 13, 41, 111–13, 115–16
information 28, 34, 37, 40–41, 75, 86, 116
joint statements 47–48, 56
community 107; *see also* East Asian Community
community-building 21, 24
concept of 8, 15, 23
in China 2, 5, 106
international community 21, 23, 30, 45, 48–49, 52, 62, 101, 114
security policy community (in US) 71, 85–86
strategic studies community 114
competition 3, 6, 8–9, 14, 16–17, 21, 23, 26, 28, 62–64, 70–72, 74, 77–78, 98n22, 102–103, 106, 108
military competitor 77, 87
'peer competitor' 6, 70, 78
potential competitor 26, 71, 91
'concert of powers', concept of a 5, 62–65, 82–83
confidence 53–54, 60–70, 73, 79
confidence-building measures 3, 5, 12–14, 33, 38, 76, 96
cooperation 14, 21, 24–30, 33–36, 38–41, 45, 47, 50, 52, 61–63, 72, 93, 101–102, 105, 113–19
China-Japan cooperation 113, 116
China-South Korea cooperation 50
China-US cooperation 104–105, 108, 118
cooperation goals 40
cooperation measures 40, 116
cultural cooperation 34–35, 41–42
economic cooperation 8, 16, 22, 28, 34–35, 40, 42, 54, 60–62, 85, 102
international cooperation 23, 38, 115, 117
multilateral cooperation 38, 40, 114
security cooperation 11–14, 16, 33–34, 36, 40–42, 118–19
US-Japan Security Consultative Committee (2 plus 2) meeting (May 2007) 118

US-Taiwan military cooperation 109
(*see also* Asia-Pacific Economic
Cooperation; Council for Security
Cooperation in the Asia-Pacific;
economics: economic cooperation;
energy: energy cooperation;
security: cooperation; Shanghai
Cooperation Organisation; treaties
and declarations: *Treaty of Amity
and Cooperation*)
coordination 24–25, 27–28, 33, 35–37,
40–42, 46, 50–52, 114, 116–18
Council for Security Cooperation in the
Asia-Pacific (CSCAP) 13, 16
crime:
    drug trafficking 36–37, 40–42
    illegal immigration 36, 41, 107
    kidnapping 113
    smuggling 36, 41, 55
    transnational crime in general 14, 36,
    40–41, 119
crisis management 4, 12, 29, 46, 53, 76,
108
Cuba 105
culture 18, 35, 41, 94–96, 106, 112

decision-making 12
deterrence 7, 68, 71, 73, 76, 78–80, 91
dialogue 12, 14, 84, 111, 113–14, 116–18,
119n10
    Comprehensive Dialogue Partnerships
27
    economic dialogue 108, 113, 116
    official (Track 1) dialogue 11, 118
    security dialogue 11, 116, 118:
    trilateral security dialogue 18
    strategic dialogue 103–104, 114,
    119n9: Trilateral Strategic Dialogue
    (TSD) 16, 18, 63
    unofficial (Track 2) dialogue 11, 13,
    16, 114
Diaoyutai Islands: *see* disputes and
    conflicts: Diaoyutai Islands/Senkaku
    Islands dispute

diplomacy 7, 17, 36, 45, 47–48, 52–54,
56, 64–65, 82, 102–106; *see also*
relations: diplomatic relations
    coercive diplomacy 56
    diplomatic framework 54, 104–106
    mediation 46, 53
    preventive diplomacy 12
    soft diplomacy 29, 106
disasters:
    disaster prevention/mitigation 14,
    34, 54
    Indian Ocean Tsunami (26 December
    2004) 3, 12
    North Korean flood disaster (July
    2006) 54
    Red Cross assistance in 54
diseases 14, 119
    Acquired Immune Deficiency
    Syndrome (AIDS) 107
    counter-pandemic cooperation 61
    H1N1 influenza 95
    H5N1 influenza 95
    Severe Acute Respiratory Syndrome
    (SARS) crisis (2003) 3, 12, 29, 95
disputes and conflicts 7, 13, 17–18, 22–
23, 26, 28, 33–34, 38, 46–47, 61–63,
65, 73–76, 78, 81–82, 85, 90–91, 95,
101–104, 106–115, 117–18, 119n3,
119n7, 120n20, 120n21
    Diaoyutai Islands/Senkaku Islands
    dispute 38, 81, 118
Dulles, Allen 68

East Asia 2–3, 6–9, 12–18, 21–23, 25–26,
28–30, 33–34, 39–41, 48–51, 53, 61–
62, 67–70, 77, 79–82, 85–86, 88, 90,
92–93, 95, 103, 111, 114, 117–19
East Asia Cooperation, concept of 21–23,
25–30
East Asia Economic Community 22
East Asia Summit (EAS) 3, 8, 14–16, 21–
22, 27, 62, 114, 118
East Asian Community, concept of an
15–16, 18

East Asian Regionalism, concept of 28
East China Sea 7, 38, 103, 111–14, 117–18
East Timor 3, 12, 61
economics 6, 11, 14, 17, 22, 24, 28–29, 34–36, 40–41, 54, 56, 60, 69, 71, 74–75, 80, 82, 85, 89, 92, 98n21, 102–105, 107–108, 113, 116, 119n2, 119n7
    economic crisis 119: 1997–98 Asian financial crisis 11–12, 21, 29, 102 Carlyle Group 107: Xugong Group 107
    currency 55, 107–108
    defence expenditure 17, 88–89, 95
    economic base 28, 106–108
    economic cooperation 22, 28, 34–36, 40, 42, 48, 54–55, 61, 69, 74, 85, 102: economic engagement 18; economic partner 18, 65, 67, 79
    economic development 4, 33, 69, 76, 78–79, 93, 102–103, 107: economic reform 108
    economic integration 24, 102
    economic leverage 54
    economic sanctions 46, 56
    exports 55, 104, 108
    financial flows 36, 54
    fiscal demands 71
    free trade 16, 102, 106: Free Trade Agreement (FTA) 22, 24, 27–29; North American Free Trade Agreement (NAFTA) 22
    geo-economics 101
    global commerce 89, 103, 106
    imports 39, 55, 104
    military–economy synergy 86, 88–89
    North Korean funds 60
Einstein, Albert 95
elections 35, 72, 107, 109, 110n3, 112, 115, 120n13
    Bush/Gore election campaign (2000) 74–75
energy 4, 34, 39, 103–104, 113, 116; *see also* resources
    energy cooperation 39–40, 59, 104
    energy crisis 103, 119

energy demand 103
energy diplomacy 103–104
Energy Eastward Transportation Program 39
energy security 18, 39–40
International Energy Agency 104
environment:
    environmental protection 34, 40, 107, 116, 119
    institutional environment 14
    security environment 5, 47, 50, 73, 76–78, 87–88
    strategic environment 13–14, 29
European Union 26–28, 37, 42, 120n12
exercises and operations 37, 41, 55, 64, 76, 78–79, 90, 93–94, 110

Foley, Tod 91
forces 4, 27–28, 33, 35, 47, 67–69, 71–72, 75–80, 86–88, 94, 110; *see also* military
foreign policy 45, 53, 64, 70, 86, 89, 96, 98n21, 106
forums 3, 5, 15, 35, 61; *see also* Association of Southeast Asian Nations: ASEAN Regional Forum
France 26, 28, 67, 74
Friedberg, Aaron 90
Fulbright, William 95

Germany 26, 67, 74
    Berlin 5
global warming 95
globalisation 23, 28–29
Gluck, Carol 88

Haass, Richard 93, 96, 99n33
Haig, Alexander 83
hegemony 22, 26, 64, 70, 73, 80, 82, 85, 89, 91, 98n21, 101, 103
Hill, Christopher 5, 60
Howard, John 16–17, 63
Hu Jintao 35, 47, 53–54, 56, 97, 112, 114, 119n8, 119n10
Huntington, Samuel 15–16, 98n21

India 8, 14, 16, 25, 27–28, 30, 38, 41, 62–65, 98n21
Indian Ocean: *see* disasters: Indian Ocean Tsunami
Indonesia 4, 114
influence 3–5, 13–17, 21, 25–30, 35, 38, 46–47, 50, 52–53, 56, 62–63, 70, 78–79, 81, 86, 88, 90, 92, 97n3, 101–103, 107, 109, 111, 116–18
Institute of Southeast Asian Studies 13
integration 21, 23–25, 29–30, 49, 96, 101–102, 105
intelligence 45, 75, 109
interdependence 14, 27–28, 42, 95
interference 106–108
    non-interference 13, 105–106
intervention 61, 98n21, 105, 120n20, 120n21
    non-intervention 14
Iran 38, 41, 64, 82, 104–105
Iraq 35–36, 39, 74, 78, 90
isolationism 16, 47

Japan 2–5, 7–8, 15–18, 22, 25–27, 30, 38–39, 42, 45–48, 50–51, 53, 59, 61–65, 67–68, 76–77, 79–81, 102–104, 109–114, 116–19, 119n1, 119n6, 119n7, 120n14, 120n21
    Japanese Government 2, 7, 13, 16–18, 21, 46–51, 60–63, 65, 102, 113–15, 117–18, 120n20: Japanese Diet 111–13
    Japanese militarism 69, 119n6
    Japan's foreign relations: *see* various entries under relations
    Tokyo 18: Yasukuni Shrine 112, 114, 119n2, 119n3, 119n10, 119n11
Johnson, Robert H. 88

Kazakhstan 33–37, 39–40
Keating, Paul 16–17
Kennan, George 89–90
Kim Jong-il 47
    Kim Government 45, 48–49, 105
    visit to China (January 2006) by 54
Kissinger, Henry 83
Koizumi, Junichiro 112, 114, 119n3

Korean Peninsula 22, 49, 51, 75–77, 79, 113, 117
Kunz, Diane 89
Kyrgyzstan 33

language 18, 49, 73
Latin America 39, 70, 103
laws and regulations 36, 38, 42, 65, 86
Lewis, Kevin N. 88
Libby, Lewis 'Scooter' 72
Lord, Winston 81

Ma Ying-jeou 110n3, 120n13
Mahathir bin Mohamed 24, 28
Malaysia 14, 28, 102
Mann, James 79
Maphilindo 11
marginalisation 15–17, 25, 92
media 35–37, 55, 109, 119n11
    New York Times 72
    Washington Post 109
Memoranda of Understanding 38
Middle East 6, 33–34, 39–40, 70, 78, 102–103
military 4, 36–37, 46–47, 50, 52–53, 55–56, 60, 63, 65, 69–75, 77–80, 85–96, 106–107, 109–110, 117–18, 119n6, 120n20; *see also* forces
    capabilities 17, 67–68, 75, 80, 89, 92–93, 98n22
    development 47, 50, 76, 85–86, 88, 93–94
    expenditure 17, 88–89, 95
    policy 87–88, 92, 96
    power 6, 14, 71, 73, 75, 79, 81, 87, 110, 119n6
    presence 49, 51, 68–69, 76, 91–92
    relations: *see* relations: military relations
    threats 38, 76, 98n21
missiles 45, 56n1, 56n2, 61, 88, 109
    missile defence programs and systems 46, 59, 109
    missile tests 4, 45–47, 52–56, 56n2, 109
    Taepodong-1 and *Taepodong-2* missiles 45–47

Mitchell, Gordon R. 88
Miyamoto, Yuji 119n10
modernisation 17, 24, 29, 109–10
Mongolia 38, 41
'Monroe doctrine', Asian version of 103
Morgan Stanley & Co. 104
multilateralism 3, 18–19, 62, 96, 99n33
    multilateral institutions and processes 2–3, 7–9, 16, 34, 37–41, 47, 51, 56, 60, 73, 92, 103, 114, 118–19
    multilateral sanctions 56
Myanmar 24–25, 104–105

naval power 39, 50, 104, 110
    blue-water navy 39, 104
negotiation 4–5, 27–29, 60–61, 94, 114, 117
Nelson, Richard R. 89
Nepal 105
Network of East Asian Think Tanks 16
New Zealand 8, 27–28, 62, 68
Nigeria 104–105
non-governmental organisation (NGO) 107
norms 15, 23
    diplomatic norms 7, 56
    international norms 12, 23
    regional norms 12–13, 23, 28, 62
North Atlantic Treaty Organization (NATO) 4, 42, 67–68, 81, 109
North Korea 4–5, 30, 45–56, 60–61, 63–64, 68, 105
    and nuclear weapons 5, 12, 45–54, 56, 56n2, 59–61, 65, 82, 102–103, 106, 113, 117
    North Korean Government 4–5, 12, 45–54, 56, 59, 60–61, 105, 117
    North Korea's foreign relations: see various entries under relations
    Pyongyang 13
nuclear (see also weapons: nuclear weapons):
    Central Asian Nuclear-Free Zone program 41
    North Korean nuclear program 4–5, 12, 45–46, 48–53, 56, 59–61, 65, 102–103, 106, 113, 117
    nuclear ambitions 48, 82
    nuclear capabilities 45, 49, 51, 56, 59, 68
    nuclear facilities 46, 59
    nuclear options and strategy 72, 80, 95
    nuclear tests 4, 45–54, 56, 56n2, 60, 67, 117
    nuclear threats 80: arms race 41, 72, 74, 87–88, 96
Nye, Jr., Joseph S. 106

Obama, Barack 110n3
Obey, David R. 87
operational concepts 75, 77, 93

Pakistan 38, 41, 105
Paulson, Henry 108
People's Republic of China: see China
perceptions 11–12, 17–19, 22, 75, 86, 95, 106
Perry, William 93, 96
Persian Gulf 70, 75–76
Philippines 64, 68–69, 102
politics 6–7, 11, 27, 34, 36, 52–54, 56, 63, 67–69, 71, 73–74, 76, 78–80, 85–88, 90, 98n21, 102, 104–107, 109, 111–16, 119n2, 119n9
    'cold politics and warm economy' 113, 119n7
    Geopolitics/international politics 13, 17, 23, 50, 89, 101–102
    political order 71, 79, 89, 91, 104
    power politics 3, 15, 51
Powell, Colin 13
proliferation 41, 49, 61, 75; see also nuclear: nuclear threats; weapons: nuclear weapons
    arms control 94
    non-proliferation 46, 94
    Proliferation Security Initiative 16
prosperity 27, 29, 47, 85, 94, 98n21
public opinion 35, 48, 53, 95, 117, 119n3
Putin, Vladimir 63

regional architecture 2, 17–18, 27; see also security: architecture
regional institutions 14

'Strategic Partnership Relationship', concept of 30
relations (*see also* alliances):
   Australia-China relations 2, 17–18, 65, 97
   Australia-US relations 18
   China-ASEAN relations 29–30
   China-India relations 38, 63, 65
   China-Japan relations 7–8, 13, 15, 18, 22, 26, 30, 38, 47, 50, 63, 65, 79–81, 103, 111–19, 119n1, 119n2, 119n7, 119n8, 119n10, 120n12, 120n20: China-Japan Culture and Sports Exchange Year (2007) 112, 113
   China-North Korea relations 4, 45–56, 60–61, 79
   China-South Korea relations 47–48, 50–51, 79, 117
   China-Soviet relations 33, 79
   China–US–Taiwan relations 109
   diplomatic relations 13, 51, 56, 102, 104, 106
   economic relations 22, 105, 119n7; *see also* economics: economic cooperation
   international relations 1, 5, 7–9, 12–14, 22, 25–30, 33, 38, 42, 48, 61–64, 67, 79, 92–93, 95, 97n3, 102, 104–105, 112, 116–17
   military relations 85–86, 90, 92–93, 109, 113, 118
   security relations 14, 64, 68, 95, 97
   strategic relations 29–30, 65, 86, 101, 104–105, 111–13, 115–16
   US-China relations 6, 15, 50–51, 63–65, 68, 78–83, 85–86, 90, 92–94, 97n3, 98n22, 101–110, 114, 118, 119n1
   US–China–Japan triangle 7, 114, 118
   US-Japan relations 8, 63, 114, 118, 120n21
   US-South Korea relations 8
   US-Taiwan relations 92–93, 109
Renouf, Alan 15
resources 3, 34, 39–40, 54–55, 89, 91, 95, 97, 103–104
   oil 39–40, 49, 55–56, 70, 103–104
   Xinjiang–Shanghai Gas Pipeline 39
Rice, Condoleezza 5, 27, 107
Richardson, Dennis 17
risks 3, 29–30, 39, 41, 49, 59, 61, 70, 72–73, 80, 83, 87, 96, 101, 103–106, 108–109, 117–18
'rogue states' 78–79, 105
Rudd, Kevin 63
   Rudd Government 18
Rumsfeld, Donald 77
Russia 3–4, 8, 22, 27, 33, 35, 38–40, 59, 63–64, 81, 98n21, 104; *see also* Soviet Union

Schlesinger, James 87
Sea of Japan 56n2
security 3–4, 7, 15–17, 22–23, 28, 33, 36, 38, 41–42, 47, 50, 62–63, 71, 73, 75–77, 79–80, 85–86, 89–90, 96, 97n3, 109, 111, 114, 117–19
   affairs 37, 61, 65
   architecture 1–2, 4–5, 7–9, 11–12, 14–18, 28–29, 33, 38, 41, 51, 67, 69, 72–73, 79, 85–86, 88, 92–93, 95, 97, 118–19, 119n7: security tripod 8
   bilateral security 68
   challenges 7, 14, 25, 35–37, 52, 61, 73, 75, 79, 96, 118–19
   commitments 76
   community 24, 62, 85–86
   'comprehensive security', concept of 40, 42
   cooperation 2, 11–14, 33–34, 36, 38, 40–42, 118–19
   dialogue: *see* dialogue: security dialogue
   energy: *see* energy: energy security
   environment 5, 47, 73, 76–77, 111
   global security 69, 92–95
   guarantees 49
   'human security' 23
   information security 37, 40
   initiative 92
   issues 3, 14, 24, 36, 40, 47–48, 61, 80
   obligations 69
   order 63, 79

outcome 61
outlook 72, 77, 81
partner 65, 90, 97
policy 6, 69, 71, 75, 79, 85–86, 90, 97n3
posture 69, 79, 81
presence 80
problems 25, 64, 87
regional security 3, 5, 8–9, 11, 12, 14, 28, 34, 39, 42, 45, 50–51, 61, 65, 69, 76, 86, 95
requirements 95
relations: *see* relations: security relations
strategy 71, 76, 85, 89, 96
threats 14, 22–23, 38, 42, 76, 98n21, 119n6

Senkaku Islands: *see* disputes and conflicts: Diaoyutai Islands/Senkaku Islands dispute
Severino, Rodolfo 13
Shanghai Cooperation Organisation (SCO) 3–4, 8, 16, 33–42, 64–65
 SCO Business Council 35
 SCO Council of Member State Coordinators 42
 SCO Development Bank 35
 SCO framework 34–35, 37, 41
 SCO summit meetings: SCO Astana summit (2005) 34–37; SCO summit meeting in Tashkent, Uzbekistan (June 2004) 34; SCO summit meeting in Shanghai, China (June 2006) 34–35, 37, 40–41
Singapore 13, 21, 26, 28, 39, 69
Six-Party Talks 4–5, 8, 45–47, 51–53, 59–66, 102, 116–18
South China Sea 22, 38
South Korea 22, 27, 39, 48, 50, 63, 68–69
 South Korean Government 5, 8, 11, 22, 25, 28, 46–47, 50–51, 54, 59, 102, 117
 South Korea's foreign relations: *see* various entries under relations
 South Korea's 'peace and prosperity policy' 47

Southeast Asia 3–4, 13, 21–22, 24, 26–30, 39–41, 62, 79, 102, 104
Southeast Asia Treaty Organisation 11
sovereignty 8, 13–14, 23
Soviet Union 3–4, 33, 38, 67–70, 72, 79, 86–91, 96; *see also* Russia
space 86, 89, 94, 109–10
stability 3–7, 17, 27, 29–30, 33–34, 36, 38, 42, 45, 50, 61–62, 69, 74, 76, 82, 89, 91, 101, 106, 109, 113–16, 118, 119n1, 120n21
state-centric factors 14–15
Strait of Malacca 39
Strange, Susan 28
strategic:
 buffer 49, 52
 competition 15, 63, 103
 crossroads 79, 90, 106
 depth 72, 82, 101
 dialogue/communication/cooperation 63, 103–104, 108, 114, 119n9
 doctrine 96
 environment: *see* environment: strategic environment
 focus 53, 75, 77, 85, 92–93, 103, 108
 inputs 29
 interests 7, 24, 30, 50, 63, 65, 104, 111, 113
 objectives 40, 90, 92, 118: US strategic objectives 86–88, 90–91
 opportunities 6, 29, 106
 partnership 29–30, 65
 perceptions 75
 planning 96
 presence 27, 30
 problems 15, 53, 68, 73, 91, 93, 96, 97n3, 103, 106, 113, 115
 relations: *see* relations: strategic relations
 significance 4, 34, 38–40
 'strategic ring of encirclement' 103
 structure 27, 106
 support 2, 29
Strategic and Defence Studies Centre (SDSC) 1, 82

strategy 17, 23, 88, 97n3, 102, 105, 109
  defence strategy 25, 47, 53, 71–72, 91
  'grand strategy', concept of 69–72, 74–77, 81–82, 91, 93–94, 106
  national security strategy 71, 85–86, 89, 91, 96, 110
  regional cooperation strategy 27, 29–30, 91
  strategy of balance of powers 21–22, 24, 26–30, 82–83, 91
Sudan 105
  Darfur crisis in 104
Suharto 24
support 1, 3, 16–17, 22, 24–27, 29–30, 35–36, 41, 47–49, 53, 63, 65, 68, 73, 75, 77–78, 81, 107, 112–13, 116, 119n3
Syria 105
systems 89, 107
  defence/security system 46, 69, 80, 95, 101
  international system 6, 82, 101
  social system 75, 101, 105–106

Taiwan 7, 13, 30, 52, 68–69, 79–81, 90, 92–93, 101, 108–109, 110n3, 112–15, 118, 120n13
  Taiwan's foreign relations: *see* various entries under relations
Taiwan Strait 22, 68, 90, 92, 109, 118, 120n20, 120n21
  1995–96 Taiwan Strait crisis 12, 81
Tajikistan 33
technology 35–36, 75–78
  communication technology 116
  information technology 34
  missile technology 45
terrorism 14, 25, 33, 39, 41, 75, 78
  anti-terrorism 33, 37, 39, 41–42, 64: Regional Anti-Terrorist Structure (RATS) 34, 37, 41
  'arc of terrorism' 39
  counter-terrorism 3–4, 61, 102, 119
  cyber-terrorism 36

Shanghai Convention on Combating Terrorism, Separatism and Extremism (15 June 2001) 33
  terrorist attacks (11 September 2001) 33, 74, 77–78
  'war on terror' 3, 74, 90
terrorist groups 4, 39, 41
  Abu Sayyaf 39
  al-Qaeda 36, 39
  Hizb-ut-Tahrir (the Islamic Party of Liberation) 36
  Jemaah Islamiyah 39
  Kumpulan Mujahidin Malaysia 39
  terrorist networks 33, 39, 78–79
Thailand 68, 102
Toynbee, Arnold 94
trade: *see* economics
transformation 25, 69, 75–77, 82, 90, 107
travel: *see* visits
treaties and declarations 2, 33, 36, 40, 42n1, 63
  Australia-Japan security declaration (March 2007) 2, 17
  Nuclear Non-Proliferation Treaty 46
  security treaties 17, 22
  Treaty of Amity and Cooperation (TAC) 13, 22, 27–29
  Treaty on the Southeast Asia Nuclear Weapon Free Zone 29, 31n2
Truman, Harry S. 67

unipolarity 6, 72, 81–83
  'unipolar moment' 82
United Kingdom 15, 67
United Nations 38, 41, 56, 72, 86, 92, 94, 116
  UN Charter 94
  UN General Assembly 38
  UN reform 114, 116
  UN sanctions 48, 56, 117
  UN Security Council 48, 56, 63, 81, 94, 114, 117: UNSC Resolution 1695 45, 48; UNSC Resolution 1705 45; UNSC Resolution 1718 45

United States 1–6, 14–17, 21–22, 26–28, 30, 33, 37, 39, 42, 45, 47, 49–51, 53, 59–65, 67–76, 78–79, 81–83, 85–86, 88–90, 92–97, 98n21, 99n33, 101–109, 114, 117–18, 120n20
National Security Council (NSC): *United States Objectives and Programs for National Security* (NSC-68) (April 1950) 67–68
New York: Columbia University 88
'one China' policy of 108
Princeton University, NJ: Princeton Project on National Security 88, 96
RAND Corporation 88–89
US Congress 75, 87, 95, 108–109, 114: House Appropriations Committee 87; National Defense Panel (NDP) 75–76; US–China Economic and Security Review Commission of Congress (1 February 2007) 109
US Department of Defense: *Defense Planning Guidance* (1992) 91; *Defense Strategy for the 1990s: The Regional Defense Strategy* (1993) 72; *The United States Security Strategy for the East Asia-Pacific Region* (1998) 76
    Pentagon 68–72, 74–75, 77–78, 80–82, 86, 87–88, 90: *East Asian Strategy Report* (1998) 75; *National Security Strategy* (August 1991) 71–72
    Quadrennial Defense Reviews (QDRs) 75 (1977); 77–78 (2001); 78, 80 (2006)
US foreign relations: *see* various entries under relations
US Government 4–6, 13, 15, 18, 22, 26–27, 46–47, 49–51, 53, 59, 61, 67–69, 71, 74–76, 78–83, 86, 88–89, 91, 105–108, 114
US military/forces 4, 46–47, 49–51, 67–69, 71–72, 74–79, 81, 85–93, 96, 98n22, 108–110: US Air Force 87; US Navy 78; *see also* vessels

US policy 4–6, 16, 22, 47, 50–51, 53, 59, 64, 67–83, 85–94, 96, 97n3, 101–110: 'containment' policy of 67, 86, 108–109

Venezuela 104–105
vessels:
    Aegis cruiser 46
    aircraft carriers 78: USS *Independence* 76
    submarines 78
Vietnam 21; *see also* wars and warfare: Vietnam War
visits 7, 13, 18, 41, 54, 111, 120n12
    China-Japan exchanges 113–14, 116, 119n3, 119n10, 119n11
    visa management 55

Wang Guangya 56
wars and warfare 22, 34, 41, 68, 72, 74–78, 80, 87, 93, 98n22, 101, 109, 117; *see also* Cold War
    First World War 67
    Korean War 68, 79
    Second World War 15, 24, 67, 69, 81, 87, 89, 114
    Sino-Japanese War 102
    Vietnam War 69, 79, 110
weapons 36, 41, 72, 94; *see also* missiles
    arms embargo 120n21
    arms sales 90, 109
    nuclear weapons 45–46, 49–50, 52, 56, 59–60, 63, 65, 67, 94: plutonium extraction 60; non-nuclear weapon states 94; nuclear-weapon-free zones 29, 94; nuclear weapons programs 4, 5, 56, 60–61, 65
    uranium enrichment 60
    Weapons of Mass Destruction 36, 41, 45, 70, 75, 79
    weapons platforms/systems 93, 95
Wen Jiabao 46, 53–54, 111
    visit to Japan (April 2007) 18, 111–12
Wolfowitz, Paul 72, 91
World Trade Organization (WTO) 108

Xong Shili 85, 95

Yeo, George 26
Yew, Lee Kuan 16, 24, 28, 39, 69

Zhang Deguang 38
Zhou Enlai 83
Zoellick, Robert B. 82

www.ingramcontent.com/pod-product-compliance
Lightning Source LLC
Chambersburg PA
CBHW060947170426
43197CB00031B/2987